T0330816

KNOWLEDGE ORGANIZATIONS

What Every Manager Should Know

JAY LIEBOWITZ
TOM BECKMAN

S_L^t

St. Lucie Press

Boca Raton   Boston   London   New York   Washington, D.C.

Acquiring Editor: Drew Gierman
Project Editor: Albert W. Starkweather, Jr.
Cover design: Denise Craig

Library of Congress Cataloging-in-Publication Data

Liebowitz, Jay
    Knowledge organizations: what every manager should know / Jay Liebowitz and Thomas J. Beckman
        p. cm.
    Includes bibliographical references and index.
    ISBN 0-57444-196-5 (alk. paper)
    I. Title.
    T58.64.L54 1998
    658.4'038—dc21

                                                                    98-12630

© 1998 by Taylor & Francis Group, LLC
CRC Press is an imprint of Taylor & Francis Group, an Informa business

No claim to original U.S. Government works
International Standard Book Number 0-57444-196-5
Library of Congress Card Number 98-12630
Printed in the United States of America 1 2 3 4 5 6 7 8 9 0
Printed on acid-free paper

The Authors

Dr. Jay Liebowitz is the RWD Technologies Distinguished Professor at the University of Maryland–Baltimore County, and formerly served as Professor of Management Science in the School of Business and Public Management at George Washington University, Washington, DC. He recently served as Chaired Professor in Artificial Intelligence at the U.S. Army War College. He also was selected as the 1996 Computer Educator of the Year by the International Association for Computer Information Systems. He is the Editor-in-Chief of the international journals *Expert Systems with Applications* (Elsevier) and *Failure & Lessons Learned in Information Technology Management* (Cognizant Communication Corp.) He is the Founder and Chair of the World Congress on Expert Systems.

He can be reached at jayl@gwis2.circ.gwu.edu.

Tom Beckman served as the Chief Methodologist for the U.S. Internal Revenue Service, specializing in business reengineering, stretegic management, and knowledge management. He currently works in the Information Systems organization with the IRS, and also has a consulting company, the BekTek Group. He was educated at UCLA and MIT, and also worked in the IRS Artificial Intelligence Laboratory for a number of years. He is an adjunct faculty member at George Washington University.

He can be reached at thomas.j.beckman@ccmail.irs.gov.

Dedications

Jay would like to dedicate this book to Janet, Jason, Kenny, my parents, and all my students over the many years.

Tom would like to dedicate this book to three influences: my father, who was a knowledge sharer of the first order; my mother, who always believes in my work; and Marvin Minsky, who changed the way I think.

Preface

We now can safely say that numerous organizations have entered into the *Knowledge Age* whereby they are transforming themselves into "knowledge organizations." A knowledge organization recognizes the importance of knowledge and leverages its intellectual capital and knowledge assets of the firm, both internally and externally. The end result hopefully is a "better informed and servicing" organization whereby lessons learned, best practices, expertise, and the necessary knowledge is transferred appropriately to the employees, management, shareholders, and customers.

In this spirit, we are very proud to write this unique book on *Knowledge Organizations: What Every Manager Should Know*. This book is essential reading for managers, practitioners, senior executives, knowledge managers, chief information/knowledge officers, knowledge engineers, and IS/HRM/IT educators/students. The book covers the following areas: the Knowledge Industry, Knowledge Organizations, Intellectual Capital and Knowledge Assets, Knowledge as a Commodity, Knowledge Management, Knowledge Creation, Knowledge Repositories and Reuse, Knowledge Preservation, Sharing, and Distribution, Knowledge Valuation, Implementing the Knowledge Organization, and Future Knowledge Organizations. The book is easy-to-read, concise, and includes many vignettes and short cases of organizations involved in knowledge management. Successful organizations in the 21st century will be those who effectively can leverage their knowledge and intellectual capital. This book provides insight into how organizations can best accomplish this goal. This book is a natural follow-on to *Knowledge Management and Its Integrative Elements*, J. Liebowitz and L. Wilcox, Eds.; CRC Press, 1997.

The book is intended to be enjoyable reading that a CEO or senior manager easily can read and digest while on the airplane, at the beach, or in the study. We also have provided a number of vignettes, examples, and cases which highlight and reinforce the concepts and issues addressed in this book. These organizational examples provide a frame of reference for helping other entities become knowledge organizations.

We firmly believe that for knowledge management to be successful, the corporate culture needs to be adapted to encourage the creation, sharing, and distribution of knowledge within the organization. Knowledge repositories need to be created, managed, and maintained. Incentives for stimulating those to contribute and use the knowledge in these repositories also need to be developed. In addition, the knowledge management system should be easy enough for members at all levels of the organization to use.

We feel that our book will provide value-added information and knowledge to those who read it. We hope you find the book as enjoyable to read as it was for us to write. During this process, we owe thanks to a number of individuals and organizations. First, we need to thank our parents, families, friends, and colleagues for their support and helpful advice along the way. Second, we would like to thank the St. Lucie/CRC Press Editors and staff for believing in this important project. Third, we want to thank George Washington University, and especially the Management Science Department, for their support and encouragement. Tom would like to thank the Quality Office staff and management and the IRS for their interest and sharing. Last, we want to pay tribute to our students and those organizations listed in the book that have taken the bold steps in leading the way toward knowledge management and becoming knowledge organizations as we enter the Knowledge Age.

Jay Liebowitz
Thomas J. Beckman
Washington, DC

Contents

1 | The Knowledge Industry

Knowledge is power.

— Francis Bacon

More than Buzz Words

Ask almost any Chief Executive Officer what distinguishes his company from its competitors. The typical response is: "Our knowledge." Ask the same CEO what comprises their "knowledge assets" and "value on this knowledge", and many CEOs will have a somewhat puzzled look.

Many leading organizations are discovering they need to do a better job of capturing, distributing, sharing, preserving, securing, and valuing this precious knowledge in order to stay ahead of their competition, or at least survive. Companies like Coca-Cola, Sequent, Hewlett-Packard, Coopers, and Lybrand, and others have established new positions within their companies to oversee and better manage knowledge in their organizations. This new position often is called the "Chief Knowledge Officer", and Knowledge Analysts (like at FedEx) assist the CKO in analyzing the knowledge processes within the firm in order to improve human performance. According to *Aegiss On-Line*, the Internet Knowledge Management Magazine, CKOs are commanding annual salaries in the range of $600,000 to $1,250,000. Experienced, high-level knowledge management consultants are making $30,000 per week when consulting on the outside.

The process of managing knowledge in organizations is referred to as "Knowledge Management" or "Enterprise Knowledge Management." The focus is to provide mechanisms for building the institutional memory or "knowledge base" of the firm to better apply, share, and manage knowledge across various components in the company. Companies now are being called "knowledge organizations," as we have moved beyond managing "information" to managing "wisdom." Wisdom might be equated with information plus added value. The added value might be some rules of thumb or "heuristics" acquired from years of experience. Wisdom is the application of "knowledge" in the right settings.

1

═══════════════ VIGNETTE ═══════════════
Full Service Intranets

A Full Service Intranet is a network inside a company that links the company's people and information in a way that makes people more productive, information more accessible, and navigation through the resources and applications of the company's computing environment more seamless than ever before. The Full Service Intranet takes advantage of the family of open standards and protocols that have emerged from the Internet. Here are some examples:

- John Deere is implementing a parts database that employees can access via the intranet.
- Olivetti uses a Netscape-based intranet to create a single "virtual laboratory" that links Olivetti's research laboratories located throughout Italy and abroad.
- Electronic Arts is developing newsgroups so that teams can discuss projects and collaborate via the Web.
- HBO is publishing multimedia files on the intranet, thereby saving thousands of dollars previously incurred for printing documents, duplicating videocassettes, and distributing marketing campaign materials among 200–300 sales representatives.
- Eli Lilly uses an intranet to distribute sales information.
- Genentech provides its employees with access to information on research seminars, company announcements, building facilities, the employee directory, commuting options, and more via their intranet.
- AT&T employees can now order office supplies right from their desktops by using Netscape Navigator and a Web interface to an internal database.
- McDonnell Douglas provides its customers with proprietary technical bulletins via an extended intranet solution.

Source: Marc Andreessen and the Netscape Product Team, *The Netscape Intranet Vision and Product Roadmap*, Netscape Communications Corp., June 11, 1996.

Without such knowledge or wisdom, companies might falter into Social Darwinism where the weaker firms get eliminated. In order to best leverage knowledge or wisdom in the organization, companies are metamorphosing into "intelligent organizations." With reengineering, downsizing, rightsizing, and other "ings" in vogue, companies are looking toward maximizing their knowledge in organizations in creative and intelligent ways.

Organizations need to get on the information and knowledge superhighway in order to stay competitive. Direct marketing and improved distribution channels can be facilitated by the Internet to better target and serve customers. Additionally, many organizations are using intranets to aid in building knowledge repositories within their organization for improved sharing of knowledge and information.

=========================VIGNETTE=========================

Knowledge Management
at General Electric Company (GE) and Monsanto

At GE, the Chief Learning Officer is collecting expertise and methods to help develop best practices that can be shared throughout the company. The Chairman and CEO, John Welch, and his corporate staff set the pace for the 12 independent Fortune 500 businesses within GE by sharing their knowledge of the best and the worst of what people are doing in each business. GENet, a corporate intranet at GE, is viewed as a primary vehicle for managing knowledge and encouraging the exchange of information and knowledge on which GE prides itself.

At Monsanto Co., their Director of Knowledge Management noted dramatic changes due to the establishment of a Knowledge Management Architecture (KMA). KMA addresses knowledge management from the perspective of creating value. Monsanto's goal is creating "insight" that is manifested in the ways Monsanto provides goods and services. The KMA approach includes a learning map that identifies questions answered and resulting decisions made, an information map that specifies the kind of information that users need; and a knowledge map that explains what users do with specific information. The knowledge map represents the conversion of information to insight or knowledge.

Source: Rebecca Barclay, "Leading the Knowledge Enterprise — CIOs, CLOs, CKOs and beyond," *KM Metazine*, 1996.

An ongoing challenge to management is applying available technology to meet the strategic goals of the organization. Improved customer service, faster response times for customer transactions, enhanced worker productivity, more just-in-time planning, and improved quality control are examples of objectives where technology can be used to achieve the intended purposes by the organization. In addition to managing technology, overcoming cultural barriers in doing business also will continue to be an important ingredient towards the success of the organization.

The Knowledge Society

Today society is increasingly predicated on knowledge. There are different types of knowledge.

Procedural Knowledge deals with "how to" knowledge, actionable application of knowledge.

Declarative Knowledge deals with descriptive, "what to do" information.

Episodic Knowledge uses similarity based or analogical reasoning whereby previous episodes, events, or cases are stored, matched, and retrieved for application to new situations.

Heuristic Knowledge relates to rules of thumb developed through experience. These "informed shortcuts" help to separate the experts from the novices.

Meta-Knowledge deals with controlling reasoning or knowledge about knowledge, and deciding when to invoke the other types of knowledge. Metaknowledge is a higher level of abstraction or sophistication compared with episodic, procedural, and declarative knowledge.

Society is comprised of a collection of these various types of knowledge. In societal terms, procedural knowledge could pertain to the goods sector whereby various procedural steps in manufacturing goods are applied. Declarative knowledge could relate to the service sector whereby the service industries are based upon context-dependent, descriptive knowledge. Episodic knowledge is well-suited for the help desk sectors where a case base is populated with cases for application to a new situation or problem. Metaknowledge in societal terms relates to knowing when to apply certain knowledge in the case of schools and education for example. Heuristic knowledge deals with finding those hidden pearls of wisdom that separates the leading organizations from the laggards.

═══════════════ **VIGNETTE** ═══════════════

Example of Episodic Knowledge and Analogical Reasoning

Software Productivity Research introduced its SPR KnowledgePlan software estimation tool. The tool's Project Wizard leads software managers through a planning environment for managing small or large projects using a simple "sizing by analogy" as an alternative to more complicated metrics. It provides an extensive knowledge base of more than 6,700 projects representing all major software environments. The knowledge base is updated annually and incorporates adjustment factors on personnel, process, technology, and environment that have the most impact on project performance.

Source: "Software Estimation Tool," *IEEE Computer,* IEEE Computer Society, February 1997.

Organizations are looking for ways to capture, harness, and apply these types of knowledge internal to their organization. Some companies are developing corporate knowledge bases whereby knowledge is categorized and encoded according to the strategic mission of the firm. For example, a number of industry and government agencies have a "Lessons Learned" Department that compiles critical success/failure factors and organizational case studies/projects so a knowledge repository can be built on lessons learned. This knowledge repository can be accessed on-line to assist managers and senior executives in developing new initiatives without running into pitfalls learned from previous endeavors. This knowledge repository serves as the institutional memory of the organization, and is the mechanism for sharing and preserving knowledge throughout the organization.

The "knowledge society" is global, transcending national borders and territories. With the popularity of the World Wide Web and Internet, as the backbone, information can be obtained from almost anywhere in the world at almost any time. Intelligent search agents can easily retrieve information in efficient and effective ways. This ease of accessibility to the Web is wonderful, but the validity of some information obtained from the Web is suspect. The information or knowledge contained in web sites needs to be verified and may be inaccurate. Sharing this unverified information, therefore, needs to be carefully considered.

===============VIGNETTE===============

Yahoo! Inc. — A Knowledge Company

The CEO of Yahoo! Inc., Jerry Yang, has one of the most popular internet search companies on the web. His friend and co-founder David Filo just began compiling favorite web sites and basically just shared the knowledge with users of the web. "Knowing" what peoples' interests were helped Yahoo! Inc. grow into a billion dollar business. It's a simple concept, but one that is in good demand daily. At 28, Jerry Yang is one of the youngest and richest CEOs around.

Source: Chen, L., "Power Brokers 1996," *A. Magazine,* December 1996.

As the knowledge society continues to develop, various ethical, privacy, and security concerns surface. For example, unauthorized access to one's credit card number via electronic commerce may be a concern by many individuals. Selling of one's personal information without consent for marketing mailing lists should be a violation of rights. As the electronic age becomes more automated, ethical concerns about having automated machines replace human decisions arise. Will computers supplant human decisions and responsibilities? Who is ultimately to blame if "computerized" decisions prove incorrect? Will humans always have the final say? Who is to say that we are right more times than a computer? These questions and others will surface as artificial intelligence pervades the "knowledge society."

The selling of knowledge can certainly be considered as a "knowledge industry." In fact, the selling of knowledge has been on-going for many years. Some may say that the payment to a physician who diagnoses you is a form of selling knowledge. The physician is using his/her knowledge to analyze and treat you, and you are paying for this knowledge as a service. Even the deceitful selling of knowledge from one country's intelligence agency to another can be part of this knowledge industry as well. Knowledge is also sold as "how to" books, seminars, and courses.

In essence, the knowledge "industry" has existed for a very long time. However, now this knowledge is placed in different media forms — electronic help desks, knowledge-based and expert systems, intelligent multimedia software, virtual reality programs, advanced computer simulations, CD ROMs, digital video, and other digitized forms. Today's knowledge bases have grown immensely and rapidly, almost no matter what the discipline or domain. For example, NASA predicts that more scientific data will be sent down to Earth from the EOS (Earth Observatory System) satellites in one day than all the data sent from the previous satellites launched in their lifetime. Today's disciplines, like medicine, have become so specialized because of the vast amount of knowledge, and newly created knowledge, that the generalist (or general practitioner in medical terms) is almost obsolete. The rate of growth of new knowledge in various fields has increased so dramatically that it often is difficult to keep up with the latest advances. For example, keeping pace with new technologies, hardware, software, and techniques in the computer field is an arduous task. Recently, a supercomputer was developed by Intel and the Department of Energy that can process 1 trillion calculations in one second. This is equivalent to 667 million instructions being processed in the time it takes a speeding bullet to travel one foot. This ultra-powerful computer will be used for genetic engineering research, weather forecasting, and space research. The knowledge that can be gained from the processing of this data and information can be quite substantial.

As the half-life of knowledge and information steadily decreases over time, a great need exists to capture this knowledge in repositories so that this knowledge doesn't vanish forever. New knowledge is often created or adapted from prior or existing knowledge. Capturing and sharing this knowledge through knowledge repositories becomes a vital ingredient to an organization's success. The building of these repositories creates a new line of business for some companies. Knowledge engineering firms and artificial intelligence companies can help in acquiring, representing, and encoding the knowledge in the knowledge repositories. Creation of new opportunities for firms to construct customer knowledge repositories and other companies to develop, market, and sell "packaged" knowledge bases will be part of the growth in this knowledge industry.

=========================SIDEBAR=========================

Knowledge Reuse

"Knowledge reuse provides for the capture and reapplication of knowledge artifacts. Knowledge artifacts include episodes in memory, stories, relationships, experiences, rules of thumb, and other forms of knowledge acquired by individuals or groups. Knowledge reuse is the application of learned knowledge.

Knowledge reuse relies as much on the use of negative experiences, flawed reasoning, or wrong answers as on correct results. It is from our failures that we truly learn and so will it be with future knowledge reuse systems. Reusing knowledge will mean that we learn through others' mistakes and determine the best course of action from those mistakes" (see a new international journal called, Failure and Lessons Learned in Information Technology Management[2]).

Source: James A. King, "Software Reuse and Knowledge Reuse," *AI Expert*, Miller Freeman Publications, San Francisco, CA, April 1995.

The Knowledge Organization

In the years ahead, how can the "knowledge organization" better prepare itself for facing tomorrow's environment and marketplace? The knowledge organization will evolve from today's corporate structures into being an organization that leverages its intellectual capital. What a company knows has become as important as what it produces. According to Hewlett-Packard[1], "success in the marketplace is increasingly linked to an organization's ability to manage and leverage its intellectual capital — the intangible and often invisible assets such as knowledge and competence of people, intellectual property, and information systems that don't show up directly on the bottom line but are at least as valuable as financial assets."

According to Lewis Platt, CEO of Hewlett-Packard:[1]

> Successful companies of the 21st century will be those who do the best jobs of capturing, storing, and leveraging what their employees know.

The ability to leverage knowledge through collaboration is a major hidden value in many companies. A partnership between Hewlett-Packard and Canon has allowed a market share of 70% of the world market for laser printers.[1]

Hewlett-Packard, like other knowledge organizations, believes that intellectual property, databases, and other forms of documented learning are essential for companies to adapt to changing and growing customer needs.

VIGNETTE

Managing Knowledge at Hewlett-Packard

Hewlett-Packard is a large, successful company with more than $31 billion in 1995 revenues. Its annual revenue growth in recent years has been about 30%, and now the company competes in many markets including computers and peripheral equipment, test and measurement devices, electronic components, and medical devices. It has about 110,000 employees and more than 400 locations around the world.

One of the earliest efforts (1985) to explicitly manage knowledge at HP was a project to capture and leverage HP product knowledge for the Computer Products Organization dealer channel. Technical support for the dealer channel had previously involved answering phone calls; the business unit was growing at 40% annually, and calls from dealers were growing at the same rate. HP workers began to put frequently-asked questions on a dialup database, and the number of dealer support calls began to decline. According to David Akers, who managed the project, the development group views each support call as an error.

The system became known as HP Network News. It was converted to Lotus Notes and has been remarkably successful in reducing the number of calls. One key reason for the system's effectiveness is the developers' close attention to the actual problems faced by dealers, their customers, and not just their own ideas about what knowledge is important. Another important factor is the constant effort by developers to add value to the knowledge. For example, lists are constantly made of the most frequently asked questions, frequently encountered problems, and most popular products. These lists are publicized and dealers are encouraged to download the information from the Notes database. Less valuable information is pruned away. HP Network News is still going after 10 years, and it has been a significant factor in the high support ratings HP receives from its dealers.

Source: Thomas H. Davenport, "Knowledge Management at Hewlett-Packard, Early 1996", Graduate School of Management, University of Texas at Austin, http://knowman.bus.utexas.edu/pubs/hpcase.htm.

Leif Edvinsson, director of intellectual capital at the international insurance and financial services firm, Skandia, eloquently summarizes the importance of knowledge in organizations as follows:[1]

> Intellectual capital is at least as important as financial capital in providing an accurate picture of the enterprise's true worth. There is the part that is visible — the fruit — and the part that is hidden — the roots. If you concentrate only on the fruit and ignore the roots, the tree eventually will die. For a tree to grow and continue to produce, you must make sure that the roots are nourished. The same is true of a company. If you concentrate only on the fruit — the financial performance — and ignore the hidden values, the company will not endure over the long run.

Skandia defines intellectual capital as the gap between the market value and the book value of a company's shares. Intellectual capital is the combination of human capital and structural capital.[1] "Human capital is the knowledge, skill, and capability of individual employees to provide solutions to customers; structural capital consists of everything that remains when the employees go home (databases, customer files, software, manuals, trademarks, organizational structures, etc.)."[1]

Summary

Companies need to transform into "knowledge organizations" in order to be competitive in the evolving marketplace. Valuing intellectual capital in the organization needs to be part of the business processes in the organization. Managing knowledge and determining techniques for capturing, distributing, and sharing knowledge in the organization, will be the key ingredients to success. Incentives will need to be established to promote knowledge sharing and use. Many companies already have programs for promotion, such as Lotus which devotes 25 percent of the total performance evaluation of its employees to knowledge sharing. ABB, a top engineering company, evaluates its managers not only on the result of their decisions but also on how much knowledge and information is supplied and applied in the decision processes. Other motivational incentives such as performance evaluations, bonuses, compensation, and benefit packages could be provided based on the use and sharing of knowledge. As knowledge is continuously changing, it is necessary to dedicate and maintain a group of people (full-time) that would continuously update, and maintain the knowledge repositories, as well as validate the knowledge in the repositories. These activities should be conducted under the auspices of the CKO.

References

1. Hewlett-Packard, "Competing on Knowledge," *Fortune Magazine*, Sept. 9, 1996.
2. Liebowitz, J. (Editor-in-Chief), *Failure and Lessons Learned in Information Technology Management: An International Journal*, Cognizant Communication Corp., Elmsford, NY, 1996.

2 Knowledge Organizations

The Knowledge Organization integrates core competencies/expertise with organizational learnings, new organizational structures, and compensational schemes, and innovative information technologies to create sustainable competitive advantage.

— Tom Beckman
Implementing the Knowledge Organization in Government
presentation at the 1997 National Conference on Federal Quality

Today's and tomorrow's organizations must learn how to transform their knowledge into their most valuable asset. These "knowledge organizations" will utilize their knowledge by making it available to their employees, management, and customers. These organizations will identify the essential knowledge domains and elements within their business processes. They will determine where, when, and how to apply this knowledge, and evaluate who has and who needs the knowledge.[1] They will develop techniques for capturing, sharing, distributing, and managing knowledge.

The adage that "knowledge is power" should be embraced by organizations. Peter Drucker in "The New Society of Organizations"[2] states that "the organization's function is to put knowledge to work — on tools, products and processes, on the design of work, on knowledge itself." Many organizations are putting knowledge to work as evidenced by the following examples:[1]

- U.S. WEST is using an automated decision support system that makes product knowledge easily accessible to its home office consultants. U.S. WEST's Home Office Consulting Center increased its sales revenue per customer order by 50% and increased its customer satisfaction measurement by 20 points.

13

- Caterpillar Inc. increased its document translation capacity from two pages per hour for a single human translator to 20 pages per hour for an automated system. Caterpillar's system brings the linguistic knowledge needed for more accurate translation up to the front of the authoring process, so that documents are written in a highly translatable English.
- U.S. Army Research Laboratory demonstrated a reduction in time required to develop logistic support plans from four days to four hours. They use a knowledge-based decision support system that lets logistics planners develop the logistics support concept; analyze the effectiveness of the logistics support, and graphically visualize the logistics battlefield.
- Ford Motor Co. was able to significantly reduce its return rate for printed circuit boards by making manufacturing knowledge available to its design engineers.
- Reuters is adding value to its historical archive service offering by automatically categorizing news stories. This system now categorizes news stories 10 times faster than a human operator, with a higher level of consistency. Reuters has also established an international case base which serves as a knowledge repository for their offices worldwide. Reuters has transformed into a global knowledge organization, building knowledge bases at multiple sites around the world, and maintaining and enhancing knowledge bases within a global organizational framework.[10] This Reuter Global Case Base Project is one of the first projects to focus on building a knowledge base from expertise existing in many areas around the world. Knowledge is then distributed to multiple Reuter sites worldwide that need and want this knowledge.[10]

These are just a few examples of organizations that have placed a strong value on knowledge, and are leveraging their knowledge in efficient and productive ways.

What Makes an Organization a "Knowledge Organization"?

A "knowledge organization" is an entity that realizes the importance of its knowledge, internal and external to the organization, and applies techniques to maximize the use of this knowledge to its employees, shareholders, and customers. A critical part of being a knowledge organization is the "corporate memory" (sometimes referred to as the "organizational memory" or "knowledge repository") and the management of the knowledge within the organization (referred to as "knowledge management").

===============VIGNETTE===============

A Knowledge Organization — Buckman Laboratories

Buckman Laboratories is a $270 million company with 1,200 people in 80 countries, and makes more than 1,000 different specialty chemicals in eight factories around the world. Buckman Labs is an excellent example of a "Knowledge Organization."

Buckman began treating knowledge as their most critical corporate asset in 1992. They have become a "how-to" example in the art and science of knowledge management. Executives from AT&T, 3M, U.S. WEST, and others have visited this company to see how they manage knowledge.

Buckman uses a knowledge network called K'Netix. The ideal knowledge transfer system, according to Buckman would:

- make it possible for people to talk to each other directly, to minimize distortion.
- give everyone access to the company's knowledge base.
- allow each individual in the company to enter knowledge into the system.
- be available 24 hours a day, seven days a week.
- be easy to use.
- communicate in whatever language is best for the user.
- be updated automatically, capturing questions and answers as a future knowledge base.

According to Buckman, the real questions are: "How do we stay connected? How do we share knowledge? How do we function anytime, anywhere — no matter what?" Such a system would mean a cultural transformation.

In March 1992, Buckman set up a Knowledge Transfer Department to create the organization to manage the knowledge network. Buckman learned to effectively engage with the customer by deploying knowledge at the point of sale — to win business and to serve the customer. Knowledge sharing is power, and there need to be ways of encouraging knowledge sharing. Buckman organized an event to recognize the 150 best knowledge sharers in the company with special prizes. Buckman also learned that knowledge builds trust, and trust builds knowledge. The main lesson learned here for companies entering the knowledge economy is "What's happened here is 90% culture change. You need to change the way you relate to one another. If you can't do that, you won't succeed."

Buckman also learned about a few measurements for evaluating the performance of the knowledge network. The percentage of his workforce that is effectively engaged on the front line is a key figure. Another is education — if you want to compete on knowledge, you need to hire smart people.

Buckman realized that incorporating the knowledge transfer system into a corporate culture is at least a three-year process — "The first year they think you're crazy. The second year they start to see, and in the third year you get buy-in."

Source: Glenn Rifkin, "Buckman Labs: Nothing But Net," *Fast Company*, June/July 1996, pp. 121–127.

Corporate Memory

Corporate memory can be defined as "an explicit, disembodied, persistent representation of the knowledge and information in an organization."[3] Any piece of knowledge or information that contributes to the performance of an organization should be stored in the corporate memory. This includes knowledge about products, production processes, customers, marketing strategies, financial results, lessons learned, strategic plans and goals, and other considerations.[3] "Professional intellect"[4] of an organization should also be part of this corporate memory. Professional intellect includes:[4]

- Cognitive knowledge (know-what knowledge): basic mastery of a discipline that professionals achieve through extensive training and certification.
- Advanced skills (know-how knowledge): translates "book learning" into effective execution. The ability to apply the rules of a discipline to complex real-world problems is the most widespread value-creating professional skill level.
- Systems understanding (know-why knowledge): deep knowledge of the web of cause-and-effect relationships underlying a discipline.
- Self-motivated creativity (care-why knowledge): consists of will, motivation, and adaptability for success.

═══════════════VIGNETTE═══════════════

Transferring Knowledge to Improve Sales Productivity at KAO Systems

KAO is one of the largest outsourcing vendors of technical manufacturing services for companies like Hewlett-Packard, America OnLine, and Microsoft. Enlisting the help of Knowledge Transfer International (KTI), KAO decided to restructure its sales organization from a traditional, hierarchical operation to one of cross-functional teams that would enable individuals to expand their focus on meeting customers' needs. The team dynamic would require those with specialized areas of knowledge to become generalists. Through cross-functional teams, knowledge was transferred to improve sales productivity and resulted in a creative collaboration in meeting the customer needs.

Source: Susan Hodder, "Case Study: Cross-Functional Teams", *KM Metazine*, 1996.

Organizations that nurture care-why knowledge in their people can simultaneously thrive in the face of today's rapid changes and renew their cognitive knowledge, advanced skills, and systems understanding in order to compete in the next wave of advances.[4]

By developing a corporate memory within the organization, knowledge sharing can be facilitated as insights developed at one place in an organization are made available to other parts of the organization by storing them in a knowledge repository. Many organizations are using Lotus Notes or Intranets to facilitate the sharing of knowledge. The most suitable organization of a corporate memory depends on how the corporate memory will be used.[3] According to Heijst et al.,[4] there are four major types of corporate memories:

1. The knowledge attic
2. The knowledge sponge
3. The knowledge publisher
4. The knowledge pump

The knowledge attic is the simplest form of corporate memory management whereby the corporate memory is used as an archive which can be consulted when needed.[3] The NASA Space Engineering Lessons Learned Program is an example of the knowledge attic whereby a lessons learned database is created by completing electronic submission forms and these lessons are retrieved by completing a query form. This would be a passive collection and passive distribution effort.[3]

The knowledge sponge provides more active collection as compared with the knowledge attic corporate memory approach. Under the knowledge sponge method, the organization is actively trying to develop a more or less complete corporate memory. Whether the memory is actually used to improve the quality of the organizational processes is left to the individual workers.[3]

═══════════════════ VIGNETTE ═══════════════════

Knowledge Partnership at U.S. WEST

U.S. West has launched a "knowledge partnership group" in order to heighten the organization's interest in intellectual capital formation. This group seeks internal clients interested in knowledge transfer and sharing. The group looks for business units that have an appetite to leverage intellectual capital and facilitate collaboration. Much of the group's activity involves consulting on "culture building" — creating an environment in which employees can freely exchange information. They are trying to advocate, "sharing knowledge is power, as opposed to knowledge is power."

Source: Britton Manasco, "Leading Companies Focus on Managing and Measuring Intellectual Capital," *Knowledge Inc.,* 1996.

The knowledge publisher involves a more active distribution effort than under the knowledge attic corporate memory. Under the knowledge sponge approach, asserting lessons learned is left to the individual workers.[3] The role of the corporate memory maintainers is to analyze the lessons learned, combine these with knowledge in the corporate memory and forward them to the workers for which the lesson learned might be relevant.[3] The U.S. Department of Energy Lessons Learned Program uses this approach.

The last corporate memory classification is the knowledge pump. This is the most complex type of corporate memory involving both active collection and active distribution elements. This model emphasizes the top-down nature of organizational learning more than the other architectures.[3] The Center for U.S. Army Lessons Learned utilizes this approach.

No matter which type of corporate memory is used, the following guidelines should be strongly considered:[3]

- It should be easy for individual workers to access the knowledge in the corporate memory to facilitate individual learning from a combination of sources.
- It should be easy for workers to determine which the co-workers could have the knowledge needed for a particular activity.
- It should be easy for workers to decide which of the co-workers would be interested in a lesson learned.
- It should be easy (and rewarding) for a worker to submit a lesson learned to the corporate memory.
- There should be well-defined criteria for deciding if something is a lesson learned, how it should be formulated, and where it should be stored.
- There should be mechanisms for keeping the corporate memory consistent.
- The corporate memory should have a facility to distribute a newly asserted piece of knowledge to workers who need that knowledge.

The organization and structure of the corporate memory will be discussed in later chapters.

===============================SIDEBAR===============================

Knowledge Exchange Standard

"The Customer Support Consortium, an alliance of over 60 hardware, software, and communications companies, has published a standard for the exchange of solution information. The Solution Exchange Standard will contribute to better levels of customer support by facilitating solution exchange among vendors, outsourcers, knowledge content brokers, corporate help desks and others. Through this standard, support organizations can share information more efficiently and cost-effectively, enabling improved response to customers' increasingly complex multi-vendor support issues."

Source: "Knowledge Exchange Standard Published," *Intelligent Systems Report*, Lionheart Publishing, Atlanta, GA, June 1996.

Knowledge Management

Besides the corporate memory, knowledge organizations need to use "knowledge management" in order to manage knowledge throughout the organization.

In this sense, knowledge management serves as an organizational infrastructure that captures and leverages existing information and knowledge assets of the organization, facilitates information and knowledge dissemination across boundaries, and integrates the information and knowledge into day-to-day business processes.[5] Knowledge management involves the following knowledge processes:[3, 6–7]

- Developing New Knowledge
- Securing New and Existing Knowledge
- Distributing Knowledge
- Combining Available Knowledge

Good knowledge management involves the continuous streamlining of these processes to improve the learning capacity of the organization.[3]

Davenport[8] has developed 10 general principles of knowledge management:

1. Knowledge management is expensive (but so is stupidity!).
2. Effective management of knowledge requires hybrid solutions involving both people and technology.
3. Knowledge management is highly political.
4. Knowledge management requires knowledge managers.
5. Knowledge management benefits more from maps than models, more from markets than hierarchies.
6. Sharing and using knowledge are often unnatural acts.
7. Knowledge management means improving knowledge work processes.
8. Access to knowledge is only the beginning.
9. Knowledge management never ends.
10. Knowledge management requires a knowledge contract (i.e., intellectual property issues).

Some general principles of knowledge management are introduced above. A more detailed discussion of knowledge management will be given later in the book.

Corporate Culture

In order for a firm to become a "knowledge organization," that is a thinking, learning organization, the corporate culture needs to be conducive to such an environment. The culture of a corporation is a powerful influence in its economic performance.[11] To promote the sharing of values and knowledge, the proper organizational climate has to be created and preserved in a strategic way. Kotter and Heskett's study on corporate culture and performance, concluded the following:[12]

- Corporate culture has a significant impact on a firm's long-term economic performance.
- Corporate culture will be an even more important factor in determining the success or failure of firms in the next decade.
- Although difficult to change, management can force corporate cultures to become more performance enhancing.

Unhealthy corporate cultures typically exhibit some or all of the following:[11–12]

- Managers place a low value on the opinions and wishes of customers and stockholders.
- Managers behave insularly and politically.
- Managers place a low value on leadership and on the employees who can provide it.
- Managers tend to stifle initiative and innovation and behave in centralized and bureaucratic ways.

To create a new performance-enhancing culture (i.e., an environment in which a knowledge organization can thrive), senior leadership is essential to create a vision and a new set of strategies for the firm. This vision must be communicated by "respected" leaders in top management to managers and employees throughout the firm. Eventually, a growing coalition begins to share the values of top management, and a new corporate culture emerges. Behaviors and practices change, and once this culture is created (which can take several to many years), the culture must be preserved. Top management must communicate about the core values and behaviors and behave in ways that are consistent with that core.[11] As this continues, a new culture can be maintained to ensure that a "knowledge organization" is likely to succeed.

Summary

To be fairly called a "knowledge organization," an organization must not give merely lip service to emphasizing the value of knowledge in their organization.

Companies need to be proactive and develop a corporate memory whereby lessons learned can be captured, coordinated, and disseminated within the organization.[9] Additionally, knowledge management practices need to be carefully applied in order to leverage knowledge in the organization, and a corporate culture needs to be built and preserved to allow a knowledge organization to be established and to flourish.

How can a company become a "knowledge organization"? The following is a sample of what should be done:

- Invest in education and training of the firm's human capital.
- Develop knowledge repositories for preserving, sharing, and distributing knowledge.
- Provide incentives to encourage employees and management to contribute to the organization's knowledge repositories and use this knowledge.
- Consider evaluating annually each member of the firm on the quality and quantity of knowledge contributed to the firm's knowledge bases as well as the organizational knowledge used by that firm member.
- Develop methodologies for managing and structuring the knowledge in the knowledge repositories.
- Provide an infrastructure of individuals whose main job is to manage the creation, development, and maintenance of the knowledge repositories.
- Place the Chief Knowledge Officer (CKO) in either a staff position directly under the CEO or in a line position equivalent to a VP.
- Adapt to the changing competitive environment by forming project teams based on the employee knowledge profiles.

What are the potential drawbacks of becoming a knowledge organization? First, there may not be a guarantee of the quality, structure, and usefulness of the knowledge repositories that are created. Second, employees and management may be very reluctant to give up their competitive edge in letting others know about their shortcuts and expertise. Third, it may become unwieldy to develop and maintain these knowledge repositories. Last, security of these knowledge repositories needs to be tightly controlled so that competitors do not learn the firm's secrets.

In spite of these potential pitfalls, the advantages of being a knowledge organization and using knowledge management techniques seem to outweigh the inherent disadvantages.

════════════════ VIGNETTE ════════════════

Sportservice Corp. — A Knowledge Organization

Sportservice Corp., a ballpark food vendor, can be considered a "knowledge organization." This corporation instituted a cultural revolution to unify the home office and line business functions in order to share information more effectively. The company used information technology to lead this change, by integrating data collection and analysis across retail, food, and beverage lines of businesses. The goal was to develop a more collaborative, information sharing mindset, efficiently gather business-critical information and quickly funnel it to the people who needed it, while encouraging a more creative environment.

The Chief Information Officer (CIO) of the company integrated databases, as well as implemented an electronic brainstorming system called TeamFocus to allow groups to discuss and share information anonymously. The CIO also deployed other specific systems such as new point-of-sale systems to collect important data and then distribute it in a timely fashion to those who would analyze it, and share the findings with others.

Source: Carol Hildebrand, "Pitching Change", *CIO Magazine*, Sept. 15, 1996.

References

1. Yablonsky, D., "Reengineering Your Knowledge: Getting the Most Value for Your Most Valuable Asset," Carnegie Group, Pittsburgh, PA, http://www.cgi.com/CGI/Knowledge.html, 1996.
2. Drucker, P., "The New Society of Organizations," *Harvard Business Review*, September-October 1992, pp. 95-104.
3. Heijst, G. van, R. van der Spek, and E. Kruizinga, "Organizing Corporate Memories," University of Amsterdam, The Netherlands, 1996.
4. Quinn, J. B., P. Anderson, and S. Finkelstein, "Managing Professional Intellect: Making the Most of the Best," *Harvard Business Review*, Cambridge, MA, March-April 1996.
5. Baek, S. I. and J. Liebowitz, "An Intelligent Agent-Based Framework for Enterprise Knowledge Management," submitted to the *Expert Systems Journal*, Learned Information Ltd., 1996.

6. Wiig, K., *Knowledge Management*, Schema Press, Arlington, TX, 1993.
7. Liebowitz, J. and L. Wilcox, eds., *Knowledge Management and Its Integrative Elements*, CRC Press, Boca Raton, FL, 1997.
8. Davenport, T. H., "Some Principles of Knowledge Management", *Strategy, Management, Competition*, Winter 1996.
9. Liebowitz, J. (ed.), *Failure and Lessons Learned in Information Technology Management: An International Journal*, Cognizant Communication Corp., 3 Hartsdale Road, Elmsford, NY 10523, 1997.
10. Borron, J., D. Morales, and P. Klahr, "Developing and Deploying Knowledge on a Global Scale," *AI Magazine*, AAAI Press, Vol .17, No. 4, Winter 1996.
11. Parker, M. M., *Strategic Transformation and Information Technology*, Prentice Hall, Englewood Cliffs, NJ, 1996.
12. Kotter, J. P. and J. L. Heskett, *Corporate Culture and Performance*, The Free Press, New York, 1992.

3 | Intellectual Capital and Knowledge Assets

Knowledge management is the art of creating value from an organization's intangible assets.

— Karl Sveiby
*The New Organizational Wealth: Managing and
Measuring Knowledge Based Assets*
1997

As more organizations transform into "knowledge organizations", understanding of managing and valuing intellectual capital and knowledge assets of the organization will be heightened greatly. Many companies like GE Lighting, Xerox PARC, Hoffman-LaRoche, Ernst & Young, Gemini, McKinsey and others have created the post of Chief Knowledge Officer (CKO) or an equivalent role (i.e., Intangible Assets Director, Director of Lessons Learned, etc.) to manage the processes of capturing, distributing, and effectively using knowledge. According to Davenport,[1] the CKO must possess the following characteristics:

- Advocate or evangelist for knowledge and learning.
- Designer, implementer, and overseer of an organization's knowledge infrastructure, including its libraries, knowledge bases, human intellectual resources, computer knowledge networks, research centers, and academic relationships.
- Primary liaison between external providers of information and knowledge.
- Provider of critical input into the knowledge creation and use processes that already exist within the company, such as product development.

- Leading role in the design and implementation of a company's knowledge architectures.
- Deep experience in some aspect of knowledge management, such as its creation, dissemination, or application.
- Familiarity with knowledge-oriented companies and technologies, such as libraries and groupware.
- Ability to set a good example by displaying a high level of expertise and success.

The CKO assumes responsibility for knowledge and unstructured information and is in charge of managing those assets. These assets are often referred to as "intellectual capital," "knowledge assets," or "intangible assets."

In a survey of 226 Fortune 500 companies, undertaken by The Technology Broker,[2] 76 percent had not assigned any value in their annual report to intangible assets. Where intangible assets were included on the balance sheet, they mostly referred to goodwill written off during mergers and acquisitions.[2] Intangible assets can collectively be referred to as "intellectual capital."

According to *Fortune Magazine*,[3] intellectual capital is defined as intellectual material that has been formalized, captured, and leveraged to produce a higher-valued asset. An institute[4] working the field defines intellectual capital as the existing intellect, skills, and knowledge that the organization has the ability to deploy. The Artificial Intelligence Applications Institute[5] at the University of Edinburgh equates intellectual capital with knowledge assets which are the knowledge regarding markets, products, technologies, and organizations that a business owns or needs to own and which enable its business processes to generate profits.

The Technology Broker[2] in Cambridge, England, categorizes intellectual capital as the collective sum of human centered assets, intellectual property assets, infrastructure assets, and market assets. Human centered assets comprise the collective expertise, creative capability, leadership, entrepreneurial and managerial skills embodied by the employees of the organization. It may also include psychometric data and indicators on how individuals may perform in given situations such as high stress. Intellectual property assets include know-how, copyright, patent, design rates, trade and service marks, and other related assets. Infrastructure assets are those technologies, methodologies, and processes which enable the organization to function (e.g., methodologies for assessing risk, methods of managing a sales force, databases of information on the market or customers, etc.). Market assets represent an organization's potential due to market related intangibles (e.g., repeat business percentage, value associated with goodwill, market dominance due to the market strategy, etc.).[2]

It is argued that the intellectual capital or knowledge assets of an organization are just as important, if not more so, than its tangible assets.

Many organizations have been described by Peter Vaill of George Washington University as being "in permanent white water." With today's constant pressures of restructuring, reengineering, mergers and acquisitions, increasing competitive environments, market barriers to entry, and government regulations, organizations are facing turbulent times. Over the years, the mid-management layer in the organization has eroded, and top management loyalty can be purchased by the highest bidder almost like free agency. With this movement and the resulting loss of personal expertise, the firm's intellectual assets slowly are being depleted.

How can we replenish and harness these intellectual assets so that the organization becomes a "learning" organization? One way is to invest in human resources and bring in very talented individuals — visionaries, leaders, detailists, managers, etc. For example, Apple is wooing back Steve Jobs, one of the original founders of Apple, in order to inject some visionary ideas into Apple. Bill Gates of Microsoft believes in hiring some senior managers and executives who have gone through failures in their previous organizations. He feels that people learn more from failure than from success, and Microsoft wants to have these individuals who have experienced these failures in Microsoft's talent pool in case Microsoft faces similar problems in the future.

Another way to replenish intellectual assets is to continually develop employee capabilities. Continuing education, short courses and seminars, and formal degree programs paid by the organization can enrich the individual's assets and ultimately organizational intellectual assets as well.

Replenishing the intellectual assets can also take place through company sabbaticals, vacations, general comraderie in the firm, special events in the company, and other ways to allow the individual to feel invigorated and have enjoyment and enthusiasm in working at the organization. These activities will hopefully stimulate and enhance the creativity of the individual and improve worker productivity as well.

Managing Intellectual Capital

Managing the "knowledge resources" (i.e., intellectual assets/capital) in the organization is the process of knowledge management. Some organizations have used intranets, Lotus Notes, or World Wide Web sites for preserving and sharing knowledge in the organization. Skandia publishes an annual report on its intellectual capital. Hughes Space & Communications Co.'s "knowledge highway" includes a lessons learned database with hypertext links to directories of human expertise, published materials and other information.[6] Skandia feels that intellectual capital is the bridge between the old ways of doing things and the new ways. Skandia feels its knowledge management efforts reduced the startup time for opening a corporate office in Mexico from seven years to six months, and Steelcase cites an upswing in patent applications and a threefold increase in productivity.[6]

═══════════════════VIGNETTE═══════════════════

Managing Tacit Knowledge at the Canadian Imperial Bank of Commerce (CIBC)

Tacit knowledge determines how the organization makes decisions and shapes the collective behaviors of the members. The role of the CIBC Leadership Centre is to provide the organization with systematic practices for the generation and renewal of tacit knowledge and intellectual capital.

The renewal of tacit knowledge implies learning. At CIBC, realigning mindsets is an active management process that includes:

■ focusing the organization on the essence of its competitive advantage.
■ motivating the people by communicating the value of the target.
■ leaving room for individual and team contributions.
■ sustaining enthusiasm by providing new operational definitions as circumstances change.
■ consistently using the target and the strategies to guide resource allocation.

At CIBC, 3,200 managers have been through a program that is based on changing their mindsets from "If I give my employees half a chance, they'll do something wrong" to "If I give them half a chance, they'll do something right." Through this process, CIBC was able to go from a traditional banking culture to an inverted pyramid, customer-service culture, in 3 1/2 years. Now through the Centre, CIBC is moving from the inverted pyramid to the partnership culture.

Source: Hubert Saint-Onge, "Tacit Knowledge: The Key to the Strategic Alignment of Intellectual Capital," *Strategy & Leadership Journal,* March/April 1996.

==============================SIDEBAR==============================

Skandia Lifeline's Intellectual Capital

According to Skandia's 1996 Intellectual Capital report, the following numbers where generated for the Skandia Lifeline unit (provides health and medical insurance):

	1996
Financial Focus	
Value added/employee (SEK 000s)	3,317
Customer Focus	
Number of policyholders	71,000
Engagements/employee	59
Human Focus	
Number of employees	10
Number of leaders	1
Process Focus	
Adm. expense/gross premium (%)	21
Number of claims/claims adjuster	675
Renewal & Development Focus	
Growth in value added/employee (%)	19

Managing the intellectual capital and understanding the implications of knowledge management in an organization are not easy tasks. Of 80 corporations surveyed by Arthur Andersen during a 1995 knowledge conference, more than three-quarters called knowledge management an essential or important part of their business strategy.[6-7] But more than 90 percent admitted they hadn't yet developed reliable ways to link knowledge management to financial results.[6-7]

Valuing Intellectual Assets

Trying to determine the value of intellectual assets in an organization can be very difficult. Some companies, like the Canadian Imperial Bank of Commerce (CIBC), are considering a number of indexes to measure the growth of intellectual capital in the organization. Some measure the flow of knowledge from people (new ideas generated and implemented) to structures (new products introduced) to customers (percentage of income from new revenue streams).[3]

Other companies like NCI Research have developed a methodology for valuing intellectual capital. The steps include:[8]

Step 1: Calculate average pretax earnings for the past three years.

Step 2: Go to the balance sheet and get the average year-end tangible assets for the same three years.

Step 3: Divide earnings by assets to get the return on assets.

Step 4: For the same three years, find the industry's average ROA (return on assets).

Step 5: Calculate the "excess return." Multiply the industry-average ROA by the company's average tangible assets. Subtract that from the pretax earnings in Step One.

Step 6: Calculate the three year-average income tax rate and multiply this by the excess return. Subtract the result from the excess return to get an after-tax number — the premium attributable to intangible assets.

Step 7: Calculate the net present value of the premium. You can do this by dividing the premium by an appropriate discount rate, such as the company's cost of capital. This will yield the calculated intangible value (CIV) of the organization's intangible assets. A weak or falling CIV might be a tipoff that one's investments in intangibles aren't paying off or that one spends too much on bricks and mortar. A rising CIV can help show that a business is generating the capacity to produce future wealth.

Planning the Intellectual Capital Audit

In order to assess the structure, magnitude, and usage of intellectual capital assets in the organization, an "intellectual capital audit" should be conducted. According to Brooking,[9] there are six different types of skills required for the intellectual capital audit team:

- Corporate strategists: required to set goals and help assign high values as standards by which assets can be measured.
- Finance experts: needed for the valuation process, but these individuals must also have a knowledge of legal aspects of assets (e.g., intellectual property) in order to value them.
- Human resource experts: needed to give and evaluate occupational assessment tests and identify key skills required by the workforce in order for the organization to be able to achieve its goals.

========SIDEBAR========

Valuing Intellectual Capital at Merck

Step 1: Average pretax earnings for the past three years: $3.694 billion

Step 2: Average year-end tangible assets for the same three years: $12.953 billion

Step 3: Divide earnings by assets to get the return on assets: 29%

Step 4: For the same three years, find the industry's average return on assets: 9.9%

Step 5: Multiply the industry average return on assets by the company's average tangible assets. Subtract that from the pretax earnings in Step 1: $3.694 billion — (9.9% × $12.953 billion) = $2.41 billion

Step 6: Calculate the three year average income tax rate and multiple this by the excess return. Subtract the result from the excess return to get an after tax number — the premium attributable to intangible assets. For Merck (average tax rate: 31%), that's $1.66 billion.

Step 7: Calculate the net present value of the premium. Using a 15% discount rate, that yields, for Merck, $11.1 billion. This amount is the calculated intangible value of Merck's intangible assets. This is a measure of Merck's ability to use its intangible assets to out-perform other companies in its industry.

Another technique for calculating the "knowledge bank" is:

Defer a portion of salaries, treating it as an investment. To do this, calculate how much of an employee's work is devoted to current-year tasks and how much to seeding the future (training, planning, research, business development, etc.). Thus, all the salary of a clerk is expensed, and most of the pay of a new hire, who accomplished more learning than doing, would also be banked. In the lab, researchers' entire salaries are capitalized.

Sources: Thomas A. Stewart, "Trying to Grasp the Intangible," *Fortune*, Time Inc., Oct. 2, 1995; Thomas A. Stewart, "The Coins in the Knowledge Bank," *Fortune*, Time Inc., Feb. 19, 1996.

- Knowledge analysts: required to work with individuals in the organization to identify key knowledge assets.
- Intellectual property experts: required to assess the strength of patent and other forms of intellectual property rights protection.
- Marketing experts.

===================VIGNETTE===================

Blue Cross of Western Pennsylvania

Automated decision support can greatly reduce the burden of human cognitive overload. PlanTracker was one such knowledge-based decision support system that was used by Blue Cross of Western Pennsylvania (BCWP) for:

- significantly reducing the amount of time required to audit claims information from seven days to about one hour.
- helping BCWP to increase the frequency and volume of its records transmission process, while also reducing errors in transmitted claims data.
- allowing for a more timely and consistent billing cycle for BCWP's corporate accounts.

Since 1987, the dollar volume of claims rejected annually decreased from 10 to 4.5%. Before having PlanTracker, the previous manual system was plagued by a lack of historical information, and was ill-equipped to handle the increasingly large volume of claims data. By using PlanTracker to provide a value-added component to the existing intellectual capital at Blue Cross of Western Pennsylvania, cognitive demand on the claims analyst, due to a flood of claims data, was greatly reduced.

Source: Jerrold H. May, W. Spangler, S. Chen, and S. Donohue, "Hybrid System Improves Claims Auditing at Blue Cross," *Interfaces*, 1990.

The general process for conducting the intellectual capital audit process is:[9]

1. Identify goals, domains, and constraints.
2. Determine the optimal aspect set (where an aspect is one facet of an asset, like repeat business is an aspect of the customer base asset).

3. Assign high-values to aspects (these are the optimal states the aspect could be in, for a particular company).
4. Select the audit method (e.g., customer survey, customer interview, analysis of sales, analysis of cost of sale, market research, audit agreements, competitive analysis, determine ROI, analyze payments, etc.).
5. Audit aspects.
6. Document asset value in the intellectual capital knowledge base.

Summary

Intellectual capital is perhaps the most valuable resource in the organization. It must be treated properly and shared appropriately with others in the organization. Some obstacles still exist in building and sharing intellectual capital. Cultural barriers include: resistance to knowledge capture and reuse because of the effort required, fear of loss of privacy, fear of litigation, and fear of loss of job security,[10] as well as fear of loss of power and status. Technical barriers to building an effective organizational memory system include: how to make the knowledge capture process easy or even transparent, how to make retrieval and reuse easy or even transparent, and how to ensure relevance and intelligibility of retrieved knowledge.[10]

To summarize some intellectual capital (IC) concepts, Brooking[9] presents the following ideas:

- Enterprise = Tangible Assets + Intellectual Capital
- Intellectual Capital Sharpens the Cutting Edge
- Brands Outlive Companies
- Cherish Loyal Customers
- Position Distribution as an Asset
- Patents Protect Profits
- Intellectual Property is a Corporate Investment
- Valuable Employers and Employees Invest in Themselves
- Knowledge Rich Employees Add Value
- Protect and Grow Core Competencies
- Manage Human Resources
- Match Management Philosophy to Market Needs
- Make Corporate Culture an Asset
- Collaborate for Greater Achievements
- IT Infrastructure is Corporate Backbone

- Identify Goals, Audit Intangibles, Assess Strength
- Auditing Intellectual Capital Needs Multidisciplinary Teams
- Measurement Identifies Assets
- Know What Optimal Looks Like
- Validate the Market — Measure Market Assets
- Protect the Future — Measure Intellectual Property Assets
- Get the Right Tools — Measure Infrastructure Assets
- Grow People Power — Measure Human-Centered Assets
- Management Needs Measurement
- IC Index = Corporate Health Indicator
- Constantly Track Intellectual Capital
- Intellectual Capital = Corporate Sustainability
- Differentiate through Intangibles
- IC Management is a Continual Process
- Put Knowledge into Every Process
- Know About Your Corporate Knowledge
- Build a Corporate Memory
- Knowledge Means Power and Profits
- Keep the Innovation Wheel Turning
- IC Rich Companies Take a Long Term Perspective
- Grow Intellectual Capital for Tomorrow's Needs
- The Ability to Collaborate is an Asset
- Not all that's Valuable is Tangible
- Valuation Makes Things Valuable
- The Future is Intangible

References

1. Davenport, T., "Coming Soon: The CKO," *TechWeb*, CMP Media Inc., Sept. 5, 1994.
2. Brooking, A., *Introduction to Intellectual Capital*, The Technology Broker Ltd., Cambridge, UK, 1996.
3. Stewart, T., "Your Company's Most Valuable Asset: Intellectual Capital," *Fortune*, Oct. 3, 1994.
4. ISDW Home Page, *Intellectual Capital*, http://www.isdw.org/int.htm, 1996.
5. Artificial Intelligence Applications Institute, *Position Paper on Knowledge Asset Management*, University of Edinburgh, UK, May 28, 1996.
6. Stuart, A., "Reality Check — Knowledge Management," *CIO Magazine*, CIO Communications Inc., 1996.
7. "Elusive Assets," *CIO Magazine*, CIO Communications Inc., Nov. 15, 1995.

8. Stewart, T., "Trying to Grasp the Intangible," *Pathfinder,* Oct. 2, 1995.
9. Brooking, A., *Intellectual Capital,* International Thomson Business Press, UK, 1996.
10. Conklin, J., *Designing Organizational Memory: Preserving Intellectual Assets in a Knowledge Economy,* Corporate Memory Systems Inc., Austin, TX, 1996.

4 Knowledge as a Commodity

We're drowning in information and starving for knowledge.

— Rutherford D. Rogers
Librarian, Yale University
1985

In the previous chapter, we looked at knowledge as an asset. Can knowledge also be treated as a commodity? In the October 1996 "Survey of American Business Leaders" report on 150 chief executive opinions on information technology,[1] a growing number of executives and companies viewed the use of technology for building knowledge-based information networks as the application that will dominate in the 21st century. Fifty-two percent of the executives felt that knowledge-based information networks will dominate the application of information technology in their company's environment for the remainder of the decade. Beyond the year 2000, knowledge-based information networks are seen as growing in importance and are expected to dominate the technology environment of about two thirds of the companies surveyed. In the same report, 29 percent of the Fortune 1000 companies surveyed use information technology for communications as a means of knowledge creation and sharing information.

The key element of these executive views is treating knowledge as a valuable resource. Can this knowledge be treated as a commodity by the organization?

Knowledge as a Commodity?

According to Antonelli,[2] knowledge and information still are highly "imperfect" products from an economic point of view. Stiglitz[3] echoes this point by saying "among the commodities for which markets are most imperfect are those associated with knowledge and information." According to Cheh,[4] "some government administrators and policy makers believe that knowledge should be hoarded and traded like any other commodity ... this kind of thinking is wrong because it mistakes the profound practical differences between controlling traffic in information ideas and controlling traffic in commodities."

===== VIGNETTE =====

The Fragrance Business

"In an industrial loading area in the cold, gray drizzle, 40 miles south of London, workers in blue overalls loaded and unloaded 200-gallon steel drums of knowledge. The barrels contained a mix of specialty ingredients, designer essences a manufacturer would soon add to laundry detergent to produce a distinctive 'fragrance of spring'. If the strategy worked, 10 million consumers would desert 'air of lemon' for 'fragrance of spring' when they reached for their next box of laundry detergent. The fragrance business is ruthlessly competitive. Winning depends on knowledge: fragrance of spring was the culmination of an elaborate process of development and testing by chemists, perfumers, and chemical production engineers. Part science, part art, and a little bit of luck, the aroma was crafted by a team of industrial knowledge workers — men and women applying their special skills, their accumulated experience and knowledge of aromatics, their special noses — to the challenge of inventing the next 10 million-buyer hit."

Source: Brook Manville and Nathaniel Foote, "Strategy as If Knowledge Mattered," *FastCompany Newsletter*, 1996, http://www.fastcompany.com/fastco/Issues/Second/StratSec.htm.

Monk[5] considers the question of how can economic agents most effectively realize value from the various information and technology assets they possess? He states:[5]

"The presence of non-commodified but valuable information in the economy cannot be explained solely in terms of exchange value, as exchange valuations can only apply to items bought and sold (i.e., commodities). Instead, such information may be considered to have value in use; specifically, such information is valuable because it is or may be "used" in economic production, irrespective of whether it might have any value in exchange. Information which has value in use in production is considered here to be a resource. The same argument applies to technology: the possession of proprietary, valuable, but non-exchanged techniques by economic agents cannot be explained solely in terms of exchange values. Irrespective of how it is defined, "technology" must consist of resources rather than commodities; resources retained for their use value by firms rather than for any possible direct exchange value."

In looking at the *American Heritage Dictionary*[6] under "commodity," the following definitions are used:

1. Anything useful or that can be turned to commercial or other advantage.
2. An article of trade or commerce ... that can be transported ... .

From a purely economic view, perhaps knowledge can't be treated as a "commodity." But why can't knowledge be considered to be anything useful or that can be turned to commercial or other advantage (i.e., a commodity)?

Many companies are developing knowledge bases or knowledge publishing systems which are being mass-marketed for commercial value. For example, knowledge-based systems which tell whether power plants are adhering to the necessary government regulations and guidelines or children medical advisory systems are examples of knowledge-full systems which are being sold to the general public. The knowledge captured in the rules and heuristics of these systems is certainly something "useful" and could be applied for the advantage of its user. Knowledge repositories of "lessons learned" or "information dealing with failed projects" could be used for company and commercial gain. For example, Boeing kept a manual of lessons learned from the development of their 727 and 737 aircraft. These lessons helped in the development of future Boeing aircraft, such as the 757 and 767. If these "lessons learned" knowledge bases or knowledge repositories were sold or obtained by McDonnell Douglas (a competitor of Boeing), the commercial value of such a knowledge base could be tremendous!

According to Fox,[7] knowledge is distinct from intellect; it is acquired, rather than inborn. Personal knowledge of a company, its practices, policies, and culture, is usually critical to one's success and upward movement.[7] If this knowledge could be captured, encoded, and packaged in a format for commercial sale and value, then perhaps this knowledge could be viewed as a commodity.

═══════════════ VIGNETTE ═══════════════

Knowledge Sharing

Shared knowledge is at the core of organizational or group memory and is essential to the preservation of expertise and process knowledge. Several projects are underway that address sharing knowledge:

■ ARPA's (Advanced Research Projects Agency) Intelligent Information Services Project: Uses institutional memory tools that help organizations capture expertise and also addresses self-organizing knowledge repositories that adapt to community needs with use.

■ Stanford University's NextLink and ProcessLink Projects: Use agent-based technology to enable distributed engineering groups to coordinate design decisions through peer-to-peer communication.

■ NASA and Stanford's Generation and Conversation of Design Knowledge Project: Focuses on methodologies and tools to capture design knowledge.

Source: Daniel O'Leary, "The Internet, Intranets, and the AI Renaissance," *IEEE Computer*, IEEE Computer Society Press, January 1997.

═══════════════ SIDEBAR ═══════════════

Buying Knowledge

"Jeff Pepper, president of ServiceWare, stresses the value of buying off-the-shelf "six packs" of knowledge to get an expert system for the help desk going rapidly. In other words, why reinvent knowledge (i.e., reinventing the wheel), if you can buy knowledge for the right price?

The premise that help desks, desiring knowledge for their automated systems, should make use of pre-canned knowledge bases is a sound idea. Without the availability of knowledge to fill up their expert system shells, we will see a lot of firms toil away at trying to handcraft knowledge bases and thus NOT lead to productive use of their expert systems for a long time to come (customers don't care that the system is 'under development' — they want their knowledge NOW)."

Source: Lance B. Eliot, "The Age of Intelligent Help Desks," *Intelligent Systems Report*, Lionheart Publishing, Atlanta, GA, April 1995.

Hughes Space & Communications, the world's leading maker of commercial communications satellites, is connecting previously developed "lessons learned" databases with groupware such as Lotus Notes. This will give designers of new satellites better access to reports of defects found in earlier ones or alert them to regulatory issues earlier than now.[8] Imagine the value of these "lessons learned" knowledge bases if packaged, distributed, and bought by Hughes' competitors. On one hand, this form of knowledge could possibly be considered a "commodity." On the other hand, this knowledge could be a distinctive competency that has stratgic value and should not be sold.

According to Hayes-Roth,[9] knowledge systems are an essential weapon in the global drive for faster product development and service delivery, higher quality, and decreased costs. The economics of productivity point directly toward distributing expert knowledge on demand via high-bandwidth networks[9]. Hayes-Roth[9] envisions a wide variety of publicly available commercial services and industrial processes that exploit ubiquitous and diverse knowledge systems. Data mining tools are also being used and sold to help companies locate trends and relationships in financial databases, health care, manufacturing, production, and other fields.[10]

═══════════════════════ SIDEBAR ═══════════════════════

Best Practice Guidelines for Neural Computing

The U.K. Department of Trade and Industry (DTI) has published "Best Practice Guidelines for Developing Neural Computing Applications." DTI has found that seven out of 10 of the UK's blue chip companies are either investigating the potential of neural computing or are actually developing neural applications. To assist these companies and others, this Best Practice publication allows the sharing of lessons learned in the developing of a neural computing application, from selection and feasibility through maintenance. It is designed to help avoid potential pitfalls during the development process, provide a good framework for proper management, and develop good quality systems as efficiently and effectively as possible. Best Practice Guidelines provide sound, practical advice in an accessible format on how to conduct a neural computing application development.

Source: "Best Practice Guidelines for Neural Computing," *Expert Systems Journal*, Learned Information Ltd., Oxford, England, Vol. 12, No. 1, February 1995.

===============SIDEBAR===============

Knowledge Capital

According to knowledge strategist, Paul Strassmann of Strassmann Inc., Microsoft is especially progressive in generating and growing knowledge capital. According to Strassmann:

> Microsoft is an artist. They have generated more Knowledge Capital than anybody else I've seen recently. They do it by not only appropriating capital from their own employees, but they also use the Knowledge Capital of their customers. In 1995, it gained $8.3 billion in Knowledge Capital while expending only $3 billion for Sales, General & Administrative (SG&A). To explain Microsoft's extraordinary Overhead-to-Asset Conversion Efficiency of 277%, one has to understand that Knowledge Capital does not need to reside exclusively in the heads of employees. It also occupies the mind-share of customers who have expended their own time and money to employ Microsoft products. The company, for instance, has been able to pass on the costs of testing new software to its customers and learn from them. Microsoft understands the concept of Knowledge Capital very well.

Source: Leading Lights: Knowledge Strategist Paul Strassmann, Knowledge Inc., 1996.

Knowledge can be viewed as a commodity in many respects. Knowledge can be traded, transferred, bartered, and exchanged. Commodities can also be traded, transferred, bartered, and exchanged. Knowledge has intrinsic and extrinsic value. Commodities have mostly extrinsic value. Depending on the type of knowledge, its value either can decay rather quickly or can be a nearly everlasting truth. Similarly, some commodities, such as precious metals, also can have extended worth, while others, such as food, will degrade quickly. Knowledge can be acquired quickly or over time. Commodities can also be acquired rapidly or over time. Knowledge can be sold to the highest bidder, in the same way that commodities could be sold to the highest bidders.

An old expression is:

> Give a man a fish, he eats for a day. Teach a man to fish, he eats for a lifetime.

Giving the man a fish could be equated to giving a commodity (i.e., the fish) to a person. Teaching a man to fish is "knowledge" being taught to the man. In this sense, knowledge has more enduring value than its commodity counterpart. In this example, knowledge differs from a commodity as knowledge is more intangible and perhaps more valuable than the tangible, yet diminishing, "fish" commodity.

═══════════════ VIGNETTE ═══════════════

Teltech — A Company Putting Intellectual Capital into Practice

Teltech is a company ($17 million in revenues) based in Minneapolis whose main business is helping companies get access to external technical expertise and information. As one of its services, Teltech offers "The Expert Network." Teltech maintains a network of over 3000 experts in technical fields in their online system. These experts are typically academics, recent retirees from industry, or consultants. When a client calls Teltech, they engage in a dialogue with a Teltech "knowledge analyst" about their problem, or they are given one or more names of experts who can speak knowledgeably on the customer's issue. These names are principally found in Teltech's expert database. If the client calls the expert and has a discussion, Teltech bills the client and the expert receives a payment from Teltech.

A key premise of Teltech's business model is that people are not only guides to information, but also important repositories of expertise. Teltech uses knowledge management by having computers store databases of names and locations of individuals who have not only raw information but also experience and expertise. This model is slightly different than accomplishing knowledge management through eliciting knowledge from the minds of people to put it in computers. Teltech's business model includes the following information management innovations:

- a hybrid environment of people and technology-based services.
- pointers to people with expertise.
- mapping of information sources.
- a structure and a set of techniques for categorizing knowledge.
- focusing on the information behavior of customers.

Source: Thomas H. Davenport, *Teltech: The Business of Knowledge Management Case Study*, University of Texas at Austin, http://knowman.bus.utexas.edu/pubs/telcase.htm.

=======VIGNETTE=======

Federal Express (FedEx)

FedEx's success is not only centered around a wide array of transportation vehicles, but is due in large part to its comprehensive information network which allows the firm to track and locate the whereabouts of a package anywhere in the world at any time. Only ten minutes after a package is delivered, it is recorded in the firm's database, allowing the sending customer to confirm delivery. Such a confirmation can now be conducted via the internet, allowing customers complete freedom from burdensome telephone calls.

A futher example of FedEx's knowledge-based business is the recent development and implementation of ORION, the Optically Recorded Information Online Network. The recently designed system allows the company to scan and digitally archive paperwork, virtually eliminating any manual entry of data through a sophisticated scanning technology. It also provides secure instant access to this data and documents worldwide, and allows for instant transfer of documents otherwise handled as hard copy. The system is fully integrated into the company's human resources, finance, accounting, and operational divisions, tying the company together through a virtual web of information and knowledge. FedEx also has employed "knowledge analysts" to work in their headquarters as part of their effort to continue to be a knowledge organization.

Sources: John Conley, "Expressing It," *North American International Business Journal,* Vol. 9, No. 8, September 1996; Candler et al., "The ORION Project, Communications of the ACM," Vol. 39, No. 2, February 1996; "Snapshots", *Computerworld,* September 1996.

Summary

In the eyes of the authors, knowledge can be (and is) treated as a commodity. Knowledge has intrinsic and commercial value, and can be bartered, bought, and sold. Perhaps in the true sense of the word, knowledge may not be considered a commodity by economists. However, businesspersons and managers can easily see how knowledge can produce value-added results to an organization.

References

1. Deloitte & Touche, "Survey of American Business Leaders: Perceptions of Information Technology," *Wirthlin Worldwide*, October 1996.
2. Antonelli, C., *Economic Theory of Information Networks*, The Economics of Information Networks, C. Antonelli, ed., Elsevier, Amsterdam, 1992.
3. Stiglitz, J. E., "Markets Market Failure and Development," *American Economic Review*, May 1989.
4. Cheh, M., "Government Control of Private Ideas," *Striking a Balance: National Security and Economic Freedom*, (H. Relyea, ed.), American Association for the Advancement of Science, Washington, DC, May 1985.
5. Monk, P., "Innovation in Information Economy," *The Economics of Information Networks*, C. Antonelli, ed., Elsevier, Amsterdam, 1992.
6. *The American Heritage College Dictionary, 3rd Ed.*, Houghton Mifflin Co. Inc., Boston, MA, 1993.
7. Fox, E., *Executive Qualities*, Addison Wesley, Reading, MA, 1976.
8. Stewart, T., "Your Company's Most Valuable Asset: Intellectual Capital," *Fortune*, Oct. 3, 1994.
9. Hayes-Roth, F. and N. Jacobstein, "The State of Knowledge-Based Systems," *Communications of the ACM*, Association for Computing Machinery, March 1994.
10. Brachman, R., "Mining Business Databases," *Communications of the ACM*, Association for Computing Machinery, November 1996.

5 | Knowledge Management

Knowledge is the only instrument of production that is not subject to diminishing returns.

> — J. M. Clark, Economics professor
> Columbia University
> 1927

Building Blocks of Knowledge Organizations

Business strategy should precede and determine the necessary core competencies for the present, and set the direction for development of new core competencies for the future. These core competencies are the source of most sustainable competitive advantage. Core competencies are comprised of key capabilities, and key capabilities can be further divided into knowledge domains — disciplines and specialized subject matter areas.

It is important to be clear about the purpose behind building a Knowledge Organization. Why should you expend the resources and take such a risk? You must understand what are your core capabilities in the present and for the future. Otherwise, building a corporate memory is simply a nice academic exercise with little value-added. For each domain, an on-line electronic.

Knowledge Repository is needed to support and enable knowledge workers. Although Knowledge Repositories can be rather expensive to build and maintain, creating a Knowledge Organization can result in large gains in several areas. First, the creation of knowledge repositories and related performance support systems will greatly improve current performance. Second, creating a Knowledge Organization will greatly improve the depth of capacity, capability, and adaptability to changing conditions. Why is this important? Externally, markets, customers, products, and services are continually evolving. Internally, rapid changes in business direction are possible to respond to external threats and opportunities. Finally, creating a Knowledge Organization will change the organization in ways that will both lead and push for needed changes in the corporate culture.

The next six chapters explain in some detail what are the components of a Knowledge Organization, and how to go about constructing them. We will discuss the methods, techniques, tools, and technologies needed to create and enhance organizational knowledge and expertise. It is important to note that these components remain the same for all organizations, regardless of the industry, size, or profit status. The same holds true for the process for constructing the Knowledge Organization. Management is developed that forms the structure for Chapters 5 through 9: Identify Knowledge Domains, Collect and Select Knowledge, Organize and Store Knowledge, Share and Apply Knowledge, and Create New Knowledge.

Chapter 5 defines and describes the nature of knowledge and its relationship to information and expertise. It also describes the characteristics of expertise and defines a Knowledge Hierarchy in which the value of knowledge increases as it is transformed up the hierarchy. A formal process for Knowledge.

Chapter 6 deals with collecting and selecting existing knowledge, skills, expertise, and experience needed to support the core competencies introduced in Chapter 2, as well as how to purchase needed knowledge and expertise.

Chapter 7 describes how to establish and grow a corporate memory. This involves representing, categorizing, organizing, and integrating new knowledge into the existing corporate memory, as well as creating electronic Knowledge Repositories.

Chapter 8 deals with how to make effective use of the corporate memory through sharing and applying the knowledge. It discusses how to support performance, educate and train, and distribute and share the available knowledge and expertise.

Chapter 9 describes how to create and extract new knowledge. It covers individual and organizational learning, discovering new knowledge through experimentation, database mining, and lessons learned, as well as creative thinking and innovation. It also describes how to elicit non-verbal, unconscious knowledge from domain experts.

Chapter 10 explains the technical details in applying innovative Information Technology (IT) to implement and enable the Knowledge Organization. This is accomplished primarily through use of Artificial Intelligence disciplines such as Expert Systems, Natural Language Understanding, and Machine Learning to structure, automate, enable, and discover expertise.

Finally, in **Chapter 11** the challenging problem of implementation is tackled. A set of prerequisites are described that should be in place to greatly improve the likelihood of success. Techniques and ideas for improving leadership, culture, organizational structures, and management are developed.

The Nature of Knowledge

Before we can fully discuss the Knowledge Organization or Knowledge Management, we must agree on what knowledge is and how it differs from information or data. We propose two definitions of knowledge: one is fairly specific and practical; the other is very general.

Definition 1: Knowledge is applied information that actively guides task execution, problem-solving, and decision-making.

Definition 2: Knowledge is any text, fact, example, event, rule, hypothesis, or model that increases understanding or performance in a domain or discipline.

We will use the more inclusive definition 2 for defining "knowledge" throughout this book in a way similar to the use of the term "information."

For example, would an expert system be considered part of the information systems family?

From a business standpoint, the key questions are how much value does knowledge in a certain form provide to an organization, and how much does it cost to acquire and/or transform that knowledge? In Chapter 7 we will develop the concept of a Knowledge Hierarchy and related Knowledge Transformations in some detail:

Inputs → Data → Information → Knowledge → Expertise → Capability

Characteristics of Expertise

The difference between knowledge and expertise is a matter of degree in results and understanding. Expertise is the assessment, selection, and application of knowledge that results in consistently superior performance. It can be expressed in terms of current demonstrable performance and future potential capability.

The characteristics of expertise include fast and accurate performance, usually in a narrow domain of knowledge. In addition, an expert can explain and justify the recommendation or result, as well as explain the reasoning process leading to the result. Further, experts quickly learn from experience by avoiding previous mistakes and generally improving performance through better understanding. Expertise implies the ability to solve unique and unusual cases — often reasoning from basic principles or a model, or from a body of experience structured into cases or rules. Finally, experts often must reason under uncertainty and apply common-sense and general world knowledge to the situation at hand.

What Is Knowledge Management?

In Chapter 2, we discussed the viewpoint of several leading consultants who maintain that intellectual capital is the most important strategic asset that a company has. And these consultants further assert that intellectual capital is the primary source for creating a sustainable competitive advantage. Given its significance, intellectual capital and related knowledge need to be consciously managed to best develop and leverage their potential value to the organization.

The field of Knowledge Management is little more than 10 years old. Karl Wiig, a consultant and AI specialist, is one of the field's most prominent advocates, and is most likely the probable founder of the KM movement. He coined the term at a 1986 conference in Switzerland sponsored by the United Nations — International Labor Organization. Accordingly, we paraphrase the definition used by Dr. Wiig in a recent manuscript:[1]

Definition 1: Knowledge Management is the systematic, explicit, and deliberate building, renewal, and application of knowledge to maximize an enterprise's knowledge-related effectiveness and returns from its knowledge assets.

An alternate definition formulated by Beckman[2] that more emphasizes the potential outcomes is as follows:

Definition 2: Knowledge Management is the formalization of and access to experience, knowledge, and expertise that create new capabilities, enable superior performance, encourage innovation, and enhance customer value.

Why do we think that Knowledge Management is of critical importance in most organizations? We have seen the Industrial Age eclipsed by the Information Age between 1960 and 1990. In turn, during the 1990s, the Knowledge Age has emerged to supercede the Information Age. Much of the value-added work in enterprises today is primarily knowledge-based, and there seems to be no end in sight to this trend. For example, the work of the following functions or departments is nearly totally knowledge-based:

- Customer Service
- Information Systems
- Finance
- Human Resources/Administration
- Management

Even in manufacturing, where there is a physical product, much of the work revolves around computer-aided design and manufacturing (CAD/CAM), workflow management and just-in-time scheduling and delivery.

The Knowledge Management Process

Knowledge Management is considered a key part of the strategy to use expertise to create a sustainable competitive advantage in tomorrow's business environment. Beckman[2] has proposed a comprehensive eight-stage process for Knowledge Management:

Identify → Collect → Select → Store → Share → Apply → Create → Sell

The *Identify* stage determines which core competencies are critical to success. For example, every organization needs robust knowledge about its customers' needs and expectations, products and services, finances, processes, management, employees, and other organizational and environmental aspects. Then the related strategic capabilities and knowledge domains are identified. Knowledge domains are specialized subject matter areas where recognized experts can demonstrate superior performance. Next the existing levels of expertise in the workforce are assessed for each knowledge domain. Once the gaps between existing and needed expertise are determined, domain experts, together with training and IT professionals, can begin constructing education programs and Performance Support Systems to improve expertise levels.

The *Collect* stage deals with acquiring existing knowledge, skills, theories, and experience needed to create the selected core competencies and knowledge domains. In order to be useful, knowledge, expertise, and experience must be formalized by making it explicit. In addition, practitioners should know where and how to purchase needed knowledge and expertise in the form of databases and expert systems. In order to acquire expertise, valid knowledge sources should be identified. For example, employee suggestion programs, domain experts, and best practices databases might provide valuable sources of knowledge.

The *Select* stage takes the continuous stream of collected, formalized knowledge and assesses its value. Is there insight within the acquired information? Is this piece of knowledge already in the organizational memory? Is the acquired knowledge a new plausible domain theory that needs to be added to the Knowledge Repository? Clearly, domain experts must assess and select the knowledge to be added to the organizational memory. Without a strong filtering mechanism, the corporate memory will be nothing more than a Tower of Babel, where the valuable nuggets of knowledge are lost in a sea of information and data. However, it is important that a diversity of viewpoints from multiple domain experts be represented where appropriate. Initially, one framework should be selected as the basis for organizing and classifying knowledge to be stored in the Knowledge Repository.

The *Store* stage takes the nuggets of knowledge and classifies them and adds them to the organizational memory. This corporate memory resides in three different forms: in human minds, on paper, and electronically. Knowledge in human minds needs to be made explicit and formalized in order to be useful. What does this mean? Knowledge must be organized and represented into differing knowledge structures within a Knowledge Repository, just as data and information are organized and represented in differing types of databases. Much of this knowledge can be represented in electronic form as Expert Systems.

The *Share* stage retrieves knowledge from the corporate memory and makes it accessible to users. The workforce makes their needs and personal interests known to the corporate memory which then automatically distributes any incoming new knowledge to its "subscribers" either electronically or by paper. In addition, individuals, teams, and departments often share ideas, opinions, gossip, knowledge, and expertise in meetings held in person or through groupware. It is crucial that the potentially valuable portions of these communications, discussions, arguments, and collaborations are made available to the Capture stage of the Knowledge Management process. For example, differing points of view and their rationales should be captured as part of any decision-making process, as well as the method used to reach the final decision.

The *Apply* stage retrieves and uses the needed knowledge in performing tasks, solving problems, making decisions, researching ideas, and learning. In order to easily access, retrieve, and apply the right pieces of knowledge at the right time in the right form, more than a query language is needed. Integrated Performance Support Systems (IPSS)[28] — Winslow and Bramer, are being used by leading organizations to greatly increase the performance and capabilities of knowledge workers. First, to ease access, natural classification and navigation systems need to be built for browsing or retrieving knowledge. To retrieve just the right knowledge requires that the system understand the user's purpose and context. To receive the knowledge at the right time requires a proactive system that monitors the user's actions and determines when it is appropriate to intervene with help in the form of a job aid or training module. Users can also customize the format in which knowledge is presented. Finally, users can request reference, advisory, testing, and certification modules.

The *Create* stage uncovers new knowledge through many avenues, such as observing customers, customer feedback and analysis, causal analysis, benchmarking and best practices, lessons learned from business reengineering and process improvement projects, research, experimentation, creative thinking, and automated knowledge discovery and data mining. This stage also covers how to elicit nonverbal, unconscious knowledge from domain experts and turn it into documented formal knowledge. The key here is to make sure that these valuable new sources of knowledge and insight are formalized and captured by the Knowledge Management process, and made available to users who need the knowledge.

An eighth stage may be added, the *Sell* stage, in which new products and services are crafted from the intellectual capital that can be marketed external to the enterprise. Before this stage is possible, considerable maturity should be attained in the other seven stages. Clearly, there can be some risk to this if the new product involves substantial portions of strategic core competencies.

Characteristics of the Knowledge Organization

Over the next six chapters, we will look at many aspects of the Knowledge Organization. According to Beckman,[29] here is a summary of the most important of its characteristics:

- High Performance
- Customer-Driven
- Improvement-Driven
- Excellence-Driven
- High Flexibility and Adaptiveness
- High Levels of Expertise and Knowledge
- High Rate of Learning and Innovation
- Innovative IT-Enabled
- Self-Directed and Managed
- Proactive and Futurist

Stage 1 — Identify

The *Identify* stage addresses strategic issues such as which core competencies are critical to success. Core competencies are the bundling of expertise, tools, and methods needed to produce related strategic capabilities for a product line or service. These competencies should reflect, support, and be aligned with the business mission, values, and vision. Once core competencies have been determined, then sourcing decisions can be made. See the discussion in Chapter 6 and reference to Tobin's work in this area.[3] After sourcing decisions have been made, then those key core competencies chosen for internal development are further subdivided into Knowledge Domains.

A *Knowledge Domain* is a narrow and well-bounded speciality, field, discipline, or subject matter. When the appropriate domains are selected to support a core competency, then a capability exists. Knowledge domains provide a useful level at which to organize the enterprise not only around strucutral forms called *Centers of Expertise* (see Chapter 11 for details), but also around electronic corporate memories called Knowledge Repositories. Once established, the Identify stage, unlike stages 2–7, needs to be performed only periodically as a yearly or event-triggered review.

In addition to its strategic aspect, this stage also addresses operational issues such as whether the workforce has sufficient expertise and experience to achieve high performance. A skills assessment (a knowledge, expertise, and experience assessment in our terminology) must be conducted. There are two types of skill assessments. The operational one looks at current skills and performance to support current core competencies, and the strategic one examines what current skills can be transferred or acquired to support future core competencies.

The skills assessment process has several steps. First, the existing levels of workforce performance and expertise are determined for each Knowledge Domain. Next, the gaps between existing and needed performance and expertise are determined. Then, sourcing and development strategies can be explored. A follow-on activity of this stage involves identifying the training needs of the workforce and other enablers for high performance. To meet developmental needs, domain experts, working together with training and IT professionals, can begin building educational programs and constructing Intelligent Tutoring Systems and Integrated Performance Support Systems (see Chapter 10 for details) to improve expertise and performance levels.

What knowledge domains should be created? What capabilities need to be met? What core competencies are needed? As a starting point, human sources of expertise should be identified and shared with the rest of the organization. A simple approach is the creation of directories of expertise for each domain. Next, start building Knowledge Repositories in domains that are essential to every organization. These domains correspond to components from Beckman's Business Model for business reengineering:[30]

- **Market**   industry, competition, pricing, suppliers, distributors, partners
- **Customer**   needs, values, expectations, requirements, constraints, feedback
- **Product**   features, functionality, cost, quality
- **Service**   marketing, purchase, support and repair
- **Process**   models consist of steps with triggers, inputs, resources, outputs; and measures of cycle/work time, cost, value-added/non-value added, error/rework rate, internal and external customer satisfaction
- **Management**   business strategy, workflow/process, workforce, assets, improvement
- **Employee**   performance, skills, knowledge, career goals, interests, benefits and payroll information

If knowledge is such an important asset and commodity, how can organizations properly capture, manage, and share knowledge within (and possibly outside) the firm? According to Hubert Saint-Onge, former Director for Learning Organizations at the Canadian Imperial Bank of Commerce, leadership outcomes for organizations in the Knowledge Era should:[4]

- assemble a critical mass of capabilities to provide value-adding solutions;
- engender cooperation;
- rapidly configure/reconfigure resources, work processes, and structure around competencies and customer needs;
- team/re-team across practice fields;
- dynamically align with a shared sense of purpose and urgency;
- openly share information, knowledge, and expertise;
- promote learning, creativity, and innovation; and
- foster a culture that engenders an ethic of collaboration and interdependency.

Gordon Petrash, global director of intellectual asset and capital management for The Dow Chemical Company, echoes the previous points, and feels that intellectual assets will become a larger part of a corporation's value. He feels that intellectual asset management will be a core competency in successful corporations, and people and knowledge management processes that create learning environments will increase competitive advantage.[5] Effectively managing knowledge assets will allow some companies to move ahead of the competition. At Dow Chemical, more than 100 intellectual asset management teams, chaired by intellectual asset managers and supported by a core tech center, have already been established. Further evidence of the importance of intellectual capital or knowledge management is that the U.S. Securities and Exchange Commission and other government agencies are taking an active interest in developing "future accounting tools" and wish to have more information about a company's intellectual capital.[5] Many companies are now developing a CLO position, as Chief Learning Officer, to help organizations build their knowledge repositories for better managing knowledge.

According to the Artificial Intelligence Applications Institute at the University of Edinburgh, "knowledge management" involves the identification and analysis of available and required knowledge, and the subsequent planning and control of actions to develop knowledge assets so as to fulfil organizational objectives.[6] Knowledge management covers: identifying what knowledge assets a company possesses, analyzing how the knowledge can add value, specifying what actions are necessary to achieve better usability and added value, and reviewing the use of the knowledge to ensure added value. According to Ann Macintosh at the University of Edinburgh,[6] knowledge management is needed and important because:

- The marketplace is increasingly competitive and the rate of innovation is rising, so that knowledge must evolve and be assimilated at an ever faster rate.
- Competitive pressures are reducing the size of the workforce which holds this knowledge.
- Knowledge takes time to experience and acquire. Employees have less and less time for this.
- There are trends for employees to retire earlier and for increasing mobility, leading to loss of knowledge.
- A change in strategic direction may result in the loss of knowledge in a specific area. A subsequent reversal in policy may then lead to a

renewed requirement for this knowledge, but the employees with that knowledge may no longer be there.

For all these reasons, knowledge management is a critical part of the success of knowledge organizations. In the following sections, we will look at knowledge typology, knowledge management considerations, and potential bottlenecks.

Knowledge Typology

Many attributes of knowledge can be characterized as: messy, experiential, personal, interpersonal, tacit, intuitive, relative, connected, organic, special, and alive. In managing knowledge, the following attributes come to mind: enable, replenish, increase, map, share-broadly, access, link, customize, reflect and assimilate, and transfer.[8] Active management of this knowledge is needed to create value by capturing significant learnings, identifying opportunities to re-apply, and leveraging process.[8]

To manage knowledge, we should be aware of the various knowledge types. According to Brooking,[9] there are four conceptual levels of knowledge. These are:

1. goal-setting or idealistic knowledge
2. systematic knowledge
3. pragmatic knowledge
4. automatic knowledge

Goal-setting knowledge is "knowledge why", and we use this knowledge to identify what is possible to create our goals and values. *Systematic knowledge* is "knowledge that" where we use this knowledge to analyze a reason in depth and to synthesize new approaches and alternatives. *Pragmatic knowledge* is "knowledge-how" which is decision making and factual knowledge. *Automatic knowledge* is used to perform tasks automatically — without conscious reasoning.[9]

Much of this knowledge is "tacit" which existing only in the unconscious. There are three general types of tacit knowledge.[10] "Entrenched knowledge" can only be observed through its effect on behavior. "Articulatable knowledge" can be inferred from behavior. "Explicit knowledge" is knowledge that has already been articulated.[10]

EXAMPLES

Organizations Providing Knowledge Management Consulting

■ *Ernst & Young's Center for Business Knowledge* opened in 1994 in Cleveland, OH. More than two dozen major U.S. corporations have joined this research consortium on knowledge management.

■ *Inthesis Inc.* is a Florida-based Knowledge Management and Market Research Company specializing in competitive business information and marketplace assessment.

■ *GreenSea Consulting* provides knowledge management throughout the Internet and provides executive information systems-based solutions.

■ *Knowledge Transfer International* provides project-based knowledge management solutions to its clients.

■ *Symbolic Corp.* is building a system that allows the Customer Support Consortium, consisting of 19 companies to share advanced technical customer support via a knowledge server.

■ *Teltech Resource Network Group* provides a knowledge management service called Knowledge Commons which includes four basic services: expert networks, assisted database searches, vendor services, and technical alert services.

■ *Gutenberg Knowledge Systems* and *The ProActive Group* are two Toronto-based consulting firms which have developed the Corporate Brainscan for identifying new opportunities in the new knowledge economy.

■ *The Leadership Alliance for Organizational Learning and Knowledge Management (TLA/OLKM)* helps companies build excellence through organizational learning and systemic knowledge management.

■ *McKinsey & Co.* provides knowledge management consulting through their Director of Knowledge Management and Director of Knowledge and Practice Development.

Sources: Kazunobu Nagashima, The University of Texas at Austin, April 11, 1996, http://knowman.bus.utexas.edu/prodrev/prev_2.htm; plus Web searching.

Knowledge Management Considerations

One of the first, if not "the first", benchmark study on knowledge management was conducted by the American Productivity and Quality Center and the Global Best Practices group of Arthur Andersen.[11] This study received responses from 80 major companies, and was called the Knowledge Management Assessment Tool (KMAT). Seventy-nine percent of the respondents felt knowledge management to be central to an organization's business strategy, but 59 percent said they are doing a poor job of implementing an effective knowledge management strategy.[11]

This study recommended the integration of a knowledge management system throughout a company's entire culture rather than segregating it as a separate function. They also recommended: tearing down internal, competitive barriers to transferring knowledge between departments; finding ways to measure the benefits of knowledge management both financially and non-financially; and establishing the proper environment, values, behaviors and measurements which reward behavior for contributing instead of just taking or hoarding information and knowledge.[11]

In order to make knowledge management a reality, both people and management competencies need to be strongly considered for building organizational knowledge. Knowledge is a socially constructed phenomena, and learning requires collaboration and sharing of ideas.[14] Employees need to work together, build, and cross-fertilize the enterprise knowledge bases.[14] Management competencies need to be expanded as well to include business unit process expertise, and valuing team-based, cross-functional management. Investments in management and people renewal must be an ongoing process.[14]

Some companies, like Xerox, are trying to encourage the "distributed coffee pot" phenomenon whereby people collaborate in a virtual environment through email, Lotus Notes, groupware, and other facilitating aids. Some companies, like Andersen Consulting, are actively using tools to provide access to firmwide knowledge and experience. At Andersen, the Knowledge Xchange Knowledge Management System is used whereby more than 17,000 Andersen professionals located in 47 countries utilize the system daily to access knowledge bases, share knowledge, and communicate via email. Eventually, all 33,000 plus personnel will become system users.[15]

GTE Laboratories have introduced the idea of a CYLINA (Cyberspaced Leveraged Intelligent Agent) which is an intelligent system that gains knowledge/information through interactions with a large number of users. This system, known as Auto-FAQ (Frequently Asked Questions) also is used at GTE

Labs as a question-answering system that helps users retrieve knowledge from a large knowledge base created by CYLINA.[16] Answer Garden of MIT allows organizations to develop databases of commonly asked questions that grow "naturally" as new questions arise and are answered.[17] Ernst & Young has created a Center for Business Knowledge; Price Waterhouse has something called Knowledge View; Booz, Allen & Hamilton have Knowledge On-Line (KOL).[18] These aids allow knowledge management activities to be developed and maintained at an enterprise level.[19]

Chevron, a $32 billion enterprise operating in more than 100 countries, uses knowledge management to center on identifying and transferring best practices within the company. Chevron's corporate quality department formed a "best practices" discovery team in 1994 to locate hidden repositories of knowledge throughout the company. Chevron believes that people should share best practices, and thus published a "best practice resource map" and distributed this map to 5,000 Chevron employees. Chevron also uses intranets, groupware, data warehouses, networks, bulletin boards, and videoconferencing as key tools for storing and distributing this intelligence. Knowledge bases, lists of experts, information maps, corporate yellow pages, custom desktop applications, and other systems help knowledge workers to be more effective. In general, knowledge management tries to organize and make available important know-how, wherever and whenever it's needed. This may include processes, procedures, shortcuts, patents, reference works, formulas, best practices, forecasts, fixes, heuristics, and other types of information and knowledge.

A key issue in knowledge management and creating knowledge organizations is the reward and measurement system within the firm. According to Quinn,[20] a company needs to set up systems that use multidimensional means, such as peers and customers, to measure, appraise, and reward professional intellect. Arthur Andersen found that when they managed their branch offices as separate profit centers, they wouldn't communicate with each other. They would hold on to their information and not share it with other parts of the organization. Now, the partners share jointly in profitability and people are rewarded for posing questions and posting answers in the system.[20]

Another central issue to successful knowledge management is building a culture of a learning organization. Microsoft is building a learning organization in the sense of improving through continuous self-critiquing, feedback and sharing. Microsoft's principles toward this "learning organization" strategy are: systematically learn from past and present projects and products, encourage feedback and improvement using quantitative metrics and benchmarks, view customer support as part of the product and as data for improvement, and promote linkages and sharing across product groups.[21]

A central part of the learning organization is the creation of knowledge. Learning organizations should acquire knowledge on two levels. According to Wiig,[22] they first need to perpetually redesign their products, services, and business processes to provide acceptable deliverables to the marketplace at reasonable prices. Second, organizations need to transfer sufficient knowledge to their workforce so all can act intelligently and competently and perform the required knowledge-intensive tasks proficiently, with ease and satisfaction.[22]

Dougherty[23] suggests that many models of the learning and renewing organization do not explain "what" should be known for a particular practice nor "how" that knowledge can be created and exploited. Skandia talks about "innovation capital" as the explicit, packaged result of innovation, in the form of protected commercial rights, intellectual property, and other intangible assets and values.[24] The goal of innovation capital is to enhance rapid knowledge sharing and develop new business applications.[24] Through MIS and expert systems technologies that facilitate organizational learning, these technologies similarly enable the development of organizational intelligence and hopefully innovation.[25]

Another important aspect of knowledge management and the learning organization is to develop "knowledge profiles" of all the workers in the organization. This should be part of the corporate memory to help co-workers determine their interests in a particular lesson learned.[26] To facilitate the process of comparing knowledge items with these worker profiles, these profiles should be formulated using the same attributes and attribute values as used for the knowledge items (e.g., activities, domains, products, and services that are directly related to their jobs). [26-27] Based on their knowledge profiles, expressed interests, career goals, and organizational needs, employees also can be selected for participation in research, task forces, and project work.

═══════════════════VIGNETTE═══════════════════

KPMG Peat Marwick — The Shadow Partner and KWEB

KPMG (Peat Marwick) is one of the Big Six accounting firms. A large part of their business is to provide value-added advisory services. To help in this regard by "informating knowledge workers", the Shadow

Partner initiative was established as an online reservoir of practice and knowledge which would provide partners of the firm with universal and immediate access to both the expertise of the firm contained in internal client reports, and external expertise contained in third-party databases. The Shadow Partner concept was proven feasible in a series of technical prototypes.

The vision of the Shadow Partner was to efficiently leverage the knowledge and expertise in the firm, as codified in the various reports and documents. In addition, the Shadow Partner would make available to all partners external databases and an ability to communicate with each other any place at any time using email and voice-mail.

From the initial concept of the Shadow Partner, the next generation knowledge management environment, called KWEB, has developed. KPMG will deploy Netscape Communicator and SuiteSpot Software for KPMG's next generation knowledge management environment. According to Allan Frank, chief technology officer at KPMG, "At KPMG, our best asset is the knowledge that resides with each of our professionals. With 18,000 employees in the U.S. alone distributed across 120 offices, it's imperative that we share this knowledge to provide the best service possible to our clients. Deploying the next-generation Netscape Communicator and Netscape SuiteSpot software is part of our technology strategy to create a leading-edge knowledge sharing environment that supports our business model and enables us to share critical information around the world."

Frank also adds: "Using KWEB, project team members will be able to work on shared documents as well as send and receive Web-based mail messages, extend discussions to their partners and clients, and ultimately automate business processes. KPMG is also planning to use KWEB to hold town hall meetings over the Intranet, engage in sophisticated chat sessions and to make it easier for KPMG professionals to locate colleagues. KWEB will also serve as the front end for accessing information in legacy databases internally about particular KPMG clients and projects."

Sources: Lynda Applegate, Warren McFarlan, and James McKenney, *Corporate Information Systems Management: Text and Cases*, Irwin Publishers, Chicago, 4th Ed., 1996; Netscape Press Release, *KPMG Plans to Deploy Netscape Communicator and SuiteSpot Software for Next-Generation Knowledge Management Environment*, Jan. 24, 1997, http://home.netscape.com/newsref/pr/newsrelease325.html.

A1994 survey of 80 Dutch companies by the Knowledge Management Network,[7] indicated that:

- 80 percent of the respondents reported that there were critical business processes in which knowledge was only available to one or two persons.
- 57 percent of the respondents reported costly mistakes because that knowledge was not available at the place and/or point in time when needed.
- 52 percent of the respondents reported difficulties in securing knowledge when persons were transferred or when business processes were restructured.

Potential Bottlenecks

Developing a knowledge management infrastructure within an organization is not an easy task. People instinctively may want to withhold knowledge in order for them to not lose their sources of power and influence. Although, according to expert systems studies, experts often are willing to share their knowledge in order to free up their time to work on more difficult cases, and to pursue other professional interests.

There are a number of potential bottlenecks to building an effective organizational memory. These include cultural and technical barriers.[12] Cultural barriers include: a cultural emphasis on products and results to the exclusion of process; resistance to knowledge capture because of the effort required, the fear of loss of privacy, the fear of litigation, and the fear of loss of job security; and resistance to knowledge reuse because of the effort required and the low likelihood of finding relevant knowledge.[12] Technical barriers include: how to make the knowledge capture process easy or even transparent, how to make retrieval and reuse easy or transparent, and how to ensure relevance and intelligibility (through sufficient context) of retrieved knowledge.[12]

According to Anne Stuart of *CIO Magazine*, the pitfalls of knowledge management include:[13]

- not finding what you need when you need it (organizations must create and maintain easy-to-use "knowledge maps" or navigational tools).
- sloppy attempts at knowledge management can quickly escalate into serious information overload.
- effective knowledge management requires creating a supportive, collaborative culture that eliminates traditional rivalries.
- knowledge management could become a parody, a source of bitter internal conflict, if the resources aren't equally available enterprise-wide.

- knowledge must be strongly linked to people and processes, besides information technology.
- it's tough to translate knowledge management results to the bottom line.

Roth[14] echoes some of the above points and concludes that the primary barrier to growth in the Knowledge Age and toward strategic agility is a lack of skilled human resources and management expertise to deploy these resources. The questions will be: How do we build the thoughtware, and how do we gain the organizational knowledge?"[14] These questions will be addressed in the coming chapters.

Suggested Readings

Hamel, G. and Prahalad, C. *Competing for the Future*. Harvard Business School Press. 1994.
Leonard-Barton, D. *Wellsprings of Knowledge: Building and Sustaining the Sources of Innovation*. Harvard Business School Press. 1995.
Marquardt, M. *Building the Learning Organization*. McGraw–Hill. 1996.
Wiig, K. *Knowledge Management Foundations: Thinking about Thinking — How People and Organizations Create, Represent, and Use Knowledge*. Schema Press. 1993.
Wiig, K. *Knowledge Management: The Central Management Focus for Intelligent-Acting Systems*. Schema Press. 1994.
Wiig, K. *Knowledge Management Methods: Practical Approaches to Managing Knowledge*. Schema Press. 1995.

References

1. Wiig, K. "Knowledge Management: Where Did It Come From and Where Will It Go?" *Expert Systems with Applications*, Pergamon Press/Elsevier, Vol. 14, Fall 1997.
2. Beckman, T. *A Methodology for Knowledge Management*. International Association of Science and Technology for Development's (IASTED) International Conference on AI and Soft Computing. Banff, Canada. 1997.
3. Tobin, D. Transformational Learning: *Renewing Your Company through Knowledge and Skills*. John Wiley. 1996.
4. Saint-Onge, H., *Leading for Knowledge Value Creation*, Knowledge-Based Leadership Conference, Linkage Inc., Boston, MA, Oct. 17, 1996.
5. Petrash, G., *Managing Knowledge Assets for Value*, Knowledge-Based Leadership Conference, Linkage Inc., Boston, MA, Oct. 17, 1996.
6. Macintosh, A., *Position Paper on Knowledge Asset Management*, Artificial Intelligence Applications Institute, University of Edinburgh, Scotland, May 28, 1996, http://www.aiai.ed.ac.uk/~alm/kam.html
7. van der Spek, R. and R. de Hoog, *Tutorial on Knowledge Management*, The 3rd World Congress on Expert Systems, Seoul, Korea, February 1996.
8. Chwalek, C., *Using Technology to Leverage Human Capital*, Coopers and Lybrand, Knowledge-Based Leadership Conference, Linkage Inc., Boston, MA, Oct. 17, 1996.
9. Brooking, A., *Intellectual Capital*, International Thomson Business Press, U.K., 1996.

10. Raven, A., *The Roles of Information Technology in the Creation and Sharing of Tacit Knowledge*, International Conference on Information Systems Doctoral Colloquium, Cleveland, OH, December 1996.

11. Alonzo, E., "Best Corporate Asset: Brain Power?", *Incentive*, January 1996.

12. Conklin, J., *Designing Organizational Memory: Preserving Intellectual Assets in a Knowledge Economy*, Corporate Memory Systems Inc., Austin, Texas, 1996.

13. Stuart, A., "Reality Check — Knowledge Management," *CIO Magazine*, CIO Communications Inc., 1996.

14. Roth, A., "Achieving Strategic Agility Through Economies of Knowledge," *Strategy & Leadership*, March/April 1996.

15. Andersen Consulting, *Knowledge Xchange Knowledge Management System*, Chicago, IL, 1996, http://www.gii-awards.com/nicampgn/3556.htm.

16. Whitehead, S., "Auto-FAQ: An Experiment in Cyberspace Leveraging," *Computer Networks and ISDN Systems*, Vol. 28, 1995.

17. Ackerman, M. and T. Malone, *Answer Garden: A Tool for Growing Organizational Memory*, Proceedings of the ACM Conference on Office Information Systems, 1990.

18. Stewart, T., "Mapping Corporate Brainpower," *Fortune*, 1995.

19. Baek, S. and J. Liebowitz, "An Intelligent Agent-Based Framework for Enterprise Knowledge Management," submitted to the *Expert Systems Journal*, Learned Information, 1996.

20. Quinn, J.B., "Leveraging Intellect," *Executive Excellence*, October 1993.

21. Cusumano, M. and R. Selby, "Microsoft Secrets: How the World's Most Powerful Software Company Creates Technology, Shapes Markets, and Manages People," *The Free Press*, New York, 1995.

22. Wiig, K., *Learning Organizations in the Knowledge Society: Practical Perspectives on Knowledge and Knowledge Transfers*, Association for the Development of Computer-Based Instructional Systems Conference, Arlington, TX, Feb. 17, 1994.

23. Dougherty, D., "A Practice-Centered Model of Organizational Renewal Through Product Innovation," *Strategic Management Journal*, Vol. 13, John Wiley, 1992.

24. Skandia, *Power of Innovation: Intellectual Capital*, Supplement to Skandia's 1996 Interim Report.

25. Glynn, M.A., "Innovative Genius: A Framework for Relating Individual and Organizational Intelligences to Innovation," *Academy of Management Review*, Vol. 21, No. 4, 1996.

26. van Heijst, G., R. van der Spek, and E. Kruizinga, *Organizing Corporate Memories*, University of Amsterdam, The Netherlands, 1996.

27. Liebowitz, J. and L. Wilcox, eds., *Knowledge Management and Its Integrative Elements*, CRC Press, Boca Raton, FL, 1997.

28. Winslow, C. and Bramer, W. *Future Work: Putting Knowledge to Work in the Knowledge Economy*. Free Press. 1994.

29. Beckman, T. *Implementing the Knowledge Organization in Government* presentation. 10th National Conference on Federal Quality. 1997.

30. Beckman, T. "Expert System Applications: Designing Innovative Business Systems through Reengineering." *Handbook of Applied Expert Systems*. Liebowitz, J., ed. CRC Press. 1998.

6 Collecting and Selecting Knowledge

*The mark of a first-rate intelligence is the ability to hold two opposed ideas
in the mind at the same time and still retain the ability to function.*

— F. Scott Fitzgerald
The Crack-up
1936

Introduction

This chapter deals with the input aspects of Knowledge Management. It
consists of two stages: *Collect* and *Select*. Stage 2, Collect, discusses how to
capture existing knowledge from available internal and external sources.
Stage 3, Select, filters and assesses pieces of knowledge to determine which
pieces have value. Selected chunks of knowledge are then forwarded to the
next stage in the process, Store, that is dealt with in Chapter 7. Feedback
from the Store, Share, Apply, and Create stages are used to refine and redirect
what knowledge to capture and in what forms for the Collect stage.

Larry Kahaner[4] tells an impressive story about collecting and selecting
knowledge at Mitsubishi. Mitsubishi has about 13,000 employees into 200
offices worldwide who actively collect more than 30,000 pieces of information
daily. These data are then filtered and analyzed and later distributed to all
member companies of the Mitsubishi group. This intelligence gathering is
considered to be one of their competitive strengths.

Stage 2 — Collect

The Collect stage deals with acquiring existing knowledge, skills, theories, and experience needed to create the selected core competencies and knowledge domains. In order to be useful, knowledge, expertise, and experience must be formalized by making it explicit and capturing it electronically or on paper. In order to acquire expertise, valid knowledge sources must be identified. Much of this chapter will deal with identifying the many varied sources of knowledge that are available. In addition, we will discuss strategies for collecting knowledge, such as where and how to purchase, rent, and develop needed knowledge and expertise in the form of databases and expert systems. The Collect stage has close links with stage 7, Create, because both stages bring new knowledge into the KM process that is then fed to the Select stage. In Chapter 9, we will explain how nonverbal, unconscious knowledge can be elicited from domain experts and turned into documented formal knowledge.

Knowledge Dimensions

Knowledge can be usefully viewed from several differing perspectives. First, the degree to which knowledge is formalized is critical to the successful knowledge organization. An explicit organizational memory must be created. Second, knowledge can be organized around domains — specialized areas of knowledge, subject areas, disciplines. The power of expertise relies on the boundedness, context, structuring, and organization of knowledge provided in the narrow domains.

Third, knowledge can be divided into theoretical knowledge and practical knowledge. Practical knowledge is essential for high performance; theoretical knowledge is essential for expert understanding, progress in the discipline, and adaptability — the ability to solve difficult and unique cases. Finally, knowledge can be viewed from the maturity of the domain — the degree of structure in the knowledge. Structured knowledge exists in well-understood domains; unstructured knowledge occurs when little is known in the field and there is no underlying theoretical framework. As we shall see in Chapter 10, the degree of structure in the domain will determine which Machine Learning techniques we can apply to enrich the value of knowledge by automatically transforming it to a higher level.

Knowledge Formalization

In order for knowledge to have significant value to an organization, first it must be made public through formalization. It must be documented in an explicit form that can be understood, reviewed, shared, applied, and debated by anyone with knowledge in that domain or discipline. We will discuss these explicit forms, also called knowledge schema and representations, that knowledge can take — such as text, data, cases, and rules — in Chapter 7. Often, specialized vocabularies, jargon, and even languages exist to make domain discussions and reasoning more efficient, although this can often serve to exclude those who are not in the "know."

Sources of knowledge exist in several forms — formal, informal, and tacit. Knowledge is formalized when it is made explicit by recording it on media such as paper, video, audio, or electronic. Informal knowledge resides in the memories of humans and organizations, and can be readily accessed and communicated. Tacit sources of knowledge reside in the unconscious minds of humans and in the culture of organizations, and are therefore much more difficult to detect and elicit.

Formal knowledge has several advantages over informal and tacit knowledge. Explicit knowledge can be expressed in terms of text, images, charts, tables, and expert systems so it can be read, interpreted, discussed, and applied. In addition, formalized domain knowledge can be easily stored and distributed on paper or electronically through Knowledge Repositories. Finally, formal knowledge in symbol form can be manipulated through reasoning mechanisms to create new knowledge in the form of inferences and assertions. Often, this new explicit knowledge can be valuable.

Formal sources of knowledge relevant to the organization exist both internally and externally. Primary sources of formal knowledge internal to the organization are handbooks, manuals, forms, memos, surveys, organizational charts, measurement systems — MIS, process maps, and other forms of documentation. Primary sources of formal knowledge external to the organization are books, periodicals, journals, financial and news reporting, research findings, and industry analyses. Further external knowledge sources include the Internet, academia, conferences, trend analyses, futurists, environmental scanning, consultants, benchmarking, and best practices.

Informal knowledge should be converted into formal knowledge as soon as possible, otherwise it may be lost, just as many good ideas are forgotten because they are never written down. A verbal discussion or any audio communication that can be readily understood by someone with some domain knowledge qualifies as informal knowledge. Informal sources of knowledge include present and former employees, customers, suppliers, stakeholders, regulators, government, industry, and academia. The sources are the individual and corporate memory of facts, knowledge, and sometimes expertise that is readily available and easy to communicate or put down on paper. Informal sources include communication systems such as grapevines, observable behaviors of leaders and coworkers, and well-understood, but unwritten policies and reward systems.

Tacit Knowledge   Knowledge is considered to be tacit when it is not readily available for inspection, either through documents or discussion. In Chapter 9 we will discuss how knowledge schema and Knowledge Elicitation techniques from Artificial Intelligence and Cognitive Psychology can often extract and convert tacit cognitive knowledge into explicit knowledge. Skills and physical abilities can often be converted into explicit knowledge through observation and verbal protocols. Often it is important to internalize theoretical and other explicit knowledge into unconscious, automated behaviors for performance efficiencies. This can be accomplished through observation, practice, coaching, and apprenticing.

Tacit sources of knowledge include individual employee expertise, memories, values and beliefs; assumptions and biases; corporate culture; and social and political norms. These tacit sources are often hard to express and difficult to communicate or explain. The types of tasks involved usually include qualitative reasoning in problem-solving, decision-making, designing, and diagnoses, as well as understanding and meaning, communicating, and physical skills.

Knowledge Domains

In Chapter 5 we introduced the concept of knowledge domains. If you recall, most expertise can be organized into narrow, specialized areas of knowledge called domains. It is important to categorize knowledge into these subject areas for several reasons. First, much of the power of knowledge lies in the relationships between pieces of data, information, and knowledge. Second, otherwise there is too much knowledge available — it must be organized to be accessible. Third, by creating separate knowledge domains, it is much easier to build, enhance, and ensure the quality of such knowledge. Fourth, once classified, innovative IT, in the form of Knowledge Repositories and Performance Support Systems, can enable and leverage knowledge into capabilities and performance. Finally, a new organizational form, the Center of

Expertise, can be wrapped around each knowledge domain to support the growth and quality of its Knowledge Repository.

There are several approaches to dividing the knowledge to be contained within each Knowledge Domain. There are several dimensions along which domains can be classified:

- Disciplines or professions
- Industry
- Business system components
- Library classification scheme by subject
- Knowledge schema

Professional services firms often combine the first two dimensions. For example, these firms often bring to bear knowledge of a discipline, such as business reengineering, in conjunction with knowledge of a specific industry, such as banking, to meet customer needs in redesigning banking processes.

Industry Classification of Knowledge

- Technology
- Professional Services
- Financial Services
- Healthcare
- Transportation
- Energy
- Natural Resource
- Construction/Real Estate
- Food
- Clothing
- Travel
- Agriculture
- Government

External Components of a Business System

- Markets
- Competition
- Customers

- Products
- Services
- Suppliers

Internal Components of a Business System

- Processes
- Measures: Financials, Process, Customer, Employee, Learning/ Knowledge
- Management
- Expertise
- Technology
- Structure: Organizational, Team, and Work Role
- Motivation: Development, Empowerment, Reward
- Culture

Theory vs. Practice

Most expertise can be divided into theoretical knowledge and practical knowledge. Theoretical knowledge is comprised of the foundational concepts, principles, models, and hypotheses that have been abstracted and generalized from many years of experience and practice by leading experts in a domain. Practical knowledge is comprised of the applied theory, rules of thumb, experience, and other shortcuts that are used to achieve everyday high performance. For example, procedures provide detailed instructions on how to perform a task. Senior practitioners and experts can retrieve and apply relevant cases from their extensive experience to the situation at hand. Experts also create heuristics — rules of thumb — that they use as shortcuts to achieving fast, accurate task performance. These rule-bases are often automated into the unconscious mind for efficiency. It can be difficult to dredge up these gems into consciousness using Knowledge Elicitation techniques so that they then can be formalized.

Domain Maturity — the Degree of Structure in the Knowledge

The domain maturity is usually correlated to the degree of structure in the knowledge. The degree of structure is usually classified into three categories along a continuum:

- *Well-Structured*   Algorightms, formulas, theories, frameworks, processes — apply Model-Based Reasoning
- *Semistructured*   Judgmental, subjective, heuristics, decision rules — apply Rule-Based System
- *Unstructured*   Weak or no theory, new domain, experience is in the form of cases — apply Case-Based Reasoning.

This classification of domain maturity will help us later on when we discuss knowledge schema and apply Artificial Intelligence (AI) techniques such as Case-Based Reasoning and Machine Learning. There is also often a correlation between the certainty of the knowledge and its degree of structure. However, in noisy domains, this relationship may not hold.

Sources of Knowledge

It is essential to first capture existing knowledge that is readily available. This is where we part company with most authors and many companies who seem to believe in reinventing knowledge that is at hand. These authors and companies take an extreme view by insisting that most or all learnings must come from either personal experience or from best practices — the experience of others. Most overly focus on experiences to the exclusion of other forms of knowledge, to their great loss and missed opportunities. We believe that the so-called learning organization must be combined with existing knowledge and innovative IT to create the Knowledge Organization.

Knowledge can be acquired from a variety of external and internal sources.

External Knowledge Sources

- Publications: Current books, journals, conference proceedings, industry reports, and other periodicals
- Industry advisory services
- Industry domain experts
- Commercial databases and expert systems
- Industry conferences
- Training courses, seminars, and workshops
- Competitive intelligence
- Market feedback/data: Products and services
- Customer feedback/data: Complaints, suggestions, needs, retention

- Supplier feedback/data
- Newly hired employees
- Management consultants
- Academic research
- Benchmarking and best practices research
- Collaborations, partnerships, alliances, and joint ventures
- Environmental monitoring and scanning of events, status, and trends
  —Political
  —Government/Regulatory: laws and regulations
  —Economic
  —Social
  —Technology
  —Demographics
- Internet research
- News media: print, TV, radio

Internal Knowledge Sources

- Domain experts and senior practitioners in your organization
- Internal customers and suppliers
- Organizational assessments
- Organizational evaluations — Measurement systems and Management Information Systems:
  —Customer Satisfaction: Cost, product, service, complaints, and retention
  —Financials/Value-added
  —Process/Workflow: Productivity, quality, cost, time
  —Management
  —Learning/Expertise/Knowledge
  —Employee Satisfaction/Surveys: Quality of work life, compensation, motivation
- Process modeling and simulation
- Policies, practices, and procedures
- Internal training and education
- Business future: mission, vision, values, principles, philosophy
- Business strategy: Core competencies, resource allocation, IT, plans and forecasts

- Improvement efforts and development initiatives such as business reengineering
- Operational planning and budgeting
- Corporate governance: authority, roles and responsibilities, reporting relationships, resource allocation, and organization charts
- Organizational structure and work types
- Lessons learned and post-implementation reviews from development work: Projects, initiatives, task forces, and quality improvement efforts
- Continuous documentation of process/team work
- Employee suggestions
- Corporate newsletters

We will discuss some of the more important and topical knowledge sources in Chapters 8 and 9.

Knowledge Capture Strategies

In Chapter 2 we discussed the importance of strategic intent and identifying your company's core capabilities that align and support that direction. Next, you should decompose the core capabilities into narrower, more focused, domains of knowledge that are necessary to enable organizational performance and provide for future capabilities. In his book *Transformational Learning*, Daniel Tobin[3] suggests a three prong strategy for acquiring knowledge:

1. Buy
2. Rent
3. Develop

Buying Knowledge

He suggests three ways of buying knowledge and skills:

1. Hiring new employees with the knowledge and skills
2. Forming a partnership with another organization
3. Outsourcing a function, usually not critical, to another organization permanently

Tobin adds that hiring is especially attractive when you need expertise immediately, when the knowledge and skills are needed for the longer-term, and when knowledge and skills need to be transferred to existing employees. For example, in recent years many well-known companies have brought in new CEOs from outside their industry. These companies felt that, in addition to providing a fresh perspective, they were buying a set of knowledge and skills that would fill a strategic gap. According to McGill and Slocum,[7] for decades companies have been hiring proven learners away from other successful companies by using executive search firms. The companies hire talented performers who are also able to transfer their expertise to improve the practices of that organization.

Bob Buckman[6] seconds this: "If you want to compete on knowledge, you need to hire smart people." For example, at Buckman Labs over the past 18 years, employees with college degrees have risen from 39 to 72%. And this is in the specialty chemical industry where most knowledge is acquired on the job.

Renting Knowledge

Tobin also describes three ways of renting knowledge and skills:

1. Hiring a consultant
2. Obtaining help from customers, suppliers, academia, or professional associations
3. Subcontract work to other organizations

Renting is attractive when consultants supply proprietary methods, tools, and resources; when expertise is needed only on a one-time basis; when review and validation by a world class expert is needed; and when consultants can influence an executive decision.

Developing Knowledge

Finally, Tobin discusses four ways of developing knowledge and skills:

1. Sending employees to outside training
2. Develop and deliver in-house education and training programs
3. Hire outside trainers to do training in-house
4. Spread the resources that already exist through train-the-trainer programs

He believes developing is attractive when the expertise represents a present or future core capability, when there is a widespread, long-term need, when business improvement strategies rest primarily on knowledge and skills, and when the costs of developing employees are lower than the alternatives. We will discuss learning in more depth in Chapter 9.

Stage 3 — Select

The Select stage takes the continuous stream of collected formalized knowledge and assesses its value. This stage serves as filter, quality control, and summarizer of knowledge. Is there insight within the acquired information? Is this piece of knowledge already in the organizational memory? Is the acquired knowledge a new plausible domain theory that needs to be added to the Knowledge Repository? Clearly, domain experts must assess and select the knowledge to be added to the organizational memory.

Without a strong filtering mechanism, the corporate memory will be nothing more than a Tower of Babel, where the valuable nuggets of knowledge are lost in the sea of information and data. However, it is important that a diversity of viewpoints from multiple domain experts be represented where appropriate. Initially, one framework should be selected as the basis for organizing and classifying knowledge to be stored in the Knowledge Repository.

We believe that there are seven steps involved in selecting knowledge for future use:

1. Determine relevance and value of knowledge or information to the knowledge domain
2. Determine accuracy of knowledge
3. Identify, consolidate, and eliminate duplicate knowledge
4. Locate, develop, or create missing knowledge
5. Prove or improve likelihood of uncertain knowledge
6. Identify and resolve conflicting knowledge
7. Establish multiple frames or views for unresolvable conflicting knowledge

Knowledge Conflict and Resolution

Several authors, including van Heijst, van der Spek, and Kruizinga[5] have argued that the Corporate Memory and related Knowledge Repositories must be correct and consistent. While this seems logical at face-value, this view may be neither necessary nor desirable. For example, when domain experts have conflicting views and opinions, as well as differing theoretical frameworks, what should be done? First, bring the experts together and explore their positions using Knowledge Elicitation techniques. Very often the facilitated interaction of professionals leads to greater insights and agreement rather than impasses. At a minimum, the experts will better understand their differences, and a common working technical vocabulary can be established.

In the event that no agreement is reached, why not capture and document more than one framework? How can anyone guess which framework, or portions thereof, among several plausible candidates, is correct? Also, do you really want to risk alienating one of your true domain experts? Further, if your best domain experts are not the ones assessing and selecting the knowledge to be stored, then they should not be making such decisions. Perhaps it can be agreed that one framework or view is better suited towards novices and their development, while another perspective best serves high performance, and a third view might work best for experts in novel situations. For example, sometimes one framework will be more conceptually understandable even though it does not result in the highest performance.

Building on the AI work of Randall Davis in the program of *Teiresias* and of Politakis in the program *Seek*, Andy Trice's MIT dissertation work[8] created multiple rule-bases, each representing the expertise and opinions of differing experts. Then automated methods were developed to identify conflicts and omissions, determine which rule-bases were most correct, and to construct an improved rule-base representing the consolidated knowledge from all experts. Work by Edwina Rissland in Case-Based Reasoning at the University of Massachusetts–Amherst also can help determine the pros and cons of differing viewpoints through dialectic reasoning.

Suggested Readings

Kahaner, L. *Competitive Intelligence: From Black Ops to Boardrooms — How Businesses Gather, Analyze, and Use Information to Succeed in the Global Marketplace.* Simon & Schuster. 1996.

Leonard-Barton, D. *Wellsprings of Knowledge: Building and Sustaining the Sources of Innovation.* Harvard Business School Press. 1995.

Mabey, C. and Iles, P., ed. *Managing Learning.* Routledge. 1994.

Marquardt, M. *Building the Learning Organization.* McGraw–Hill. 1996.

Martin, J. *The Great Transition: Using the Seven Disciplines of Enterprise Engineering to Align People, Technology, and Strategy.* AMACOM. 1995.

Taylor, D. *Business Engineering with Object Technology.* John Wiley. 1995.

Tobin, D. *Transformational Learning: Renewing Your Company through Knowledge and Skills.* John Wiley. 1996.

References

1. Newell, A, and Simon, H. Human Problem Solving. Prentice Hall. 1972.

2. Beckman, T. *Applying AI to Business Reengineering.* 146 pages. ©1996. Presented at the Third World Congress on Expert Systems, Seoul, Korea, February 1996.

3. Tobin, D. *Transformational Learning: Renewing Your Company through Knowledge and Skills.* John Wiley. 1996.

4. Kahaner, L. *Competitive Intelligence: From Black Ops to Boardrooms — How Businesses Gather, Analyze, and Use Information to Succeed in the Global Marketplace.* Simon & Schuster. 1996.

5. van Heijst, G., van der Spek, R., and Kruizinga, E. "Organizing Corporate Memories." University of Amsterdam, *Social Science Informatics.* 1996.

6. Rifkin, G. "Buckman Labs: Nothing but Net." *Fast Company.* June–July 1996.

7. McGill, M. and Slocum, J. *The Smarter Organization: How to Build a Business That Learns and Adapts to Marketplace Needs.* John Wiley & Sons. 1994.

8. Trice, A. *Facilitating Consensus Knowledge Acquisition,* PhD dissertation, MIT, 1990.

7 Organizing and Storing Knowledge

The functions performed by the brain are the products of the work of thousands of different, specialized sub-systems, the intricate product of hundreds of millions of years of biological evolution.

— Marvin Minsky

Introduction

In Chapter 6, we determined which knowledge domains are important to retain and develop. We also learned where knowledge sources can be found under the Collect stage of the knowledge management process. We also explored how specialists go about deciding whether a given piece or chunk of knowledge should be selected and forwarded under the Select stage. In this chapter, we will discuss how to organize and represent the knowledge in a form from which it can be stored and easily retrieved. In the knowledge management process, this is the Store stage.

In order to understand how to create an organizational memory, we first must understand more about the nature of knowledge and how differing types of knowledge form a Knowledge Hierarchy. Next we explain how to organize and structure various types of knowledge. Then we discuss how to create an organizational memory and introduce the concept of the Knowledge Repository.

Knowledge Hierarchy

From a business standpoint, the key questions are how much value does knowledge in a certain form provide to an organization, and how much does it cost to acquire and/or transform that knowledge? For the following discussion, the narrow definition of knowledge from Chapter 5 will be used. Beckman's Knowledge Hierarchy[7] is useful in understanding the distinctions between and transformations of forms of knowledge.

Inputs → Data → Information → Knowledge → Expertise → Capability

As one moves up the Knowledge Hierarchy from data to capability, there is increasing breadth, depth, meaning, conceptualization, and value in the knowledge. The increase in value of the knowledge corresponds to the maturation of human and organizational proficiency as one moves up the Hierarchy.

Inputs consist of human knowledge and models; physical sensors, signals, and images; as well as preprocessed data, text, information, and knowledge. These inputs are detected and collected by organizational "sensors." There are a variety of input modes. Language can take form as human speech, audio signal, or printed and handwritten text on paper. Images such as charts, graphs, process maps, and product designs, are captured through printed and hand-drawn pictures, photography, as well as video. Preprocessed knowledge can take forms such as printed or online manuals, databases, and expert systems. Finally, analog and digital sensors for codes, pressure, temperature and current flows can be used to collect specialized signals such as bar-codes, touch screens, and thermometer readings.

Data are the lowest form of knowledge. Once raw inputs are captured, digitized, and converted into symbolic form as text, facts, interpreted images, and preprocessed codes, we consider them data. Data should be digitized and placed on-line as quickly as possible. Text, when referred to as a data type, does not yet have meaning, and is simply a representation consisting of characters formed into a collection of words. A fact can be a piece of information, evidence, assertion of truth or likelihood, or measurement. The most basic Knowledge Structure is the fact, consisting of an <attribute value> pair. For example, <color yellow> means the color is yellow, although we do not know to what object it refers. Images that have been interpreted have a symbolic representation. Codes are numeric values assigned to attributes, and often result from sensor measurements.

Information is data imbued with context and meaning. Information is data whose form and content are useful for a particular task after having been formalized, classified, processed, and formatted. Data models and schema have organized and transformed data into information. The nearly universal Knowledge Structure used in relational databases and Expert Systems is the entity/concept/object triple: <Object-Attribute-Value>. Continuing with our example, by providing the context of "bird," our fact now takes on new meaning:

> <bird color yellow> is understood as an observation of a yellow bird. In text, a sentence or paragraph is parsed or understood according to the definition of words, the rules of grammar, and special forms such as idiomatic phrases. Correspondingly, the text, "The bird is yellow," conveys the same meaning as <bird color yellow>. An image of a yellow bird would also convey roughly the same information. In another example, the Graphical User Interface (GUI) displays multimedia information in terms of text (commands), codes (abbreviated commands), images (icons), and sounds (alerts and errors).

Knowledge applies bodies of domain information, principles, and experience to actively guide task execution and management, decision-making, and problem-solving. There are three general types of knowledge: cases, rules, and models. There are a variety of model types such as causal, statistical, process, and procedural. Continuing our example, we might have a rule that states, "If <bird color yellow>, Then <bird type oriole>. Or we might have some convincing cases that lead us to the same conclusion or inference. As a result of our rule or cases, we have created a new piece of information, an assertion that the bird is an oriole.

Expertise applies knowledge and heuristics appropriately and efficiently to achieve fast and accurate performance under resource constraints. Experts are also able to explain, justify, and summarize their results and reasoning process. In addition, experts learn from experience and develop new heuristics, theories, and frameworks. Finally, experts can teach their knowledge, experience, and expertise to others. In our example, our ornithologist may know that there are five possible yellow birds and that we need more information in the form of another clause to assure that the bird really is an oriole: If <bird color yellow>, and If <bird location Maryland>, Then <bird type oriole>. An expert might also want to express his/her degree or lack of certainty about this conclusion by appending some numerical measure of uncertainty. For example, the conclusion might be altered into a quartel: <bird type oriole .8>, meaning that the probability is 80% that the bird is an oriole.

Capability   The highest form of knowledge is the organizational capability to perform a process, produce a product, or provide a service at a high level of performance. This large-scale achievement requires the integration, coordination, and cooperation of many individual and team effortsfrom a cluster of related knowledge domains. Capability is more than just current performance. It implies the ability to learn, to innovate and create new products and services, and to redesign and improve the processes and related business system components. Capability is also the creation and enhancement of Knowledge Repositories and Integrated Performance Support Systems through the Center of Expertise organizational form we will discuss in Chapter 11. A final return to our example might have a fully trained staff of ornithologists available to identify any type of bird on any continent at any time of day or night.

Knowledge Principles

- Explicit vs. Tacit Knowledge:
  - —Knowledge must be formalized, or made explicit, to have significant value to the organization.
  - —Only formalized knowledge can be represented electronically, and be stored, shared, and effectively applied.
- Practical vs. Theoretical Knowledge:
  - —Possessing both experiential and methodological knowledge is more valuable than either alone.
  - —Integrate practice with methods and models.
  - —"There is nothing more practical than a good theory" — Albert Einstein
- Knowledge vs. Learning:
  - —Balance collecting and organizing available knowledge with learning/creating new knowledge.
  - —The Knowledge Management Process integrates the two to create more value to the organization.
- Knowledge vs. Expertise:
  - —Knowledge is applying information and data to make valid inferences.
  - —Expertise is superior performance in reasoning using knowledge to perform tasks, solve problems, make decisions, learn new knowledge.

Organizational Memory

Corporate Memory is a catchy phrase, but what does it mean? What exactly does the organization want or need to remember? What does the organization need to know to prosper? What should be remembered, and what should be forgotten or ignored? And finally, how does an organization remember? The question of what types of knowledge an enterprise needs in order to prosper has been discussed in Chapter 6 under the Business Model and under Types of Business Knowledge. In this chapter, we will explore the last two questions.

Creating an organizational memory is central to the concept of a Knowledge Organization. Knowledge must be formalized to the maximum extent possible in order for it to be available and usable. Simply having individual employees and teams with expertise and knowledge adds little value to an organization. Knowledge in the form of human memories, skills, and emotions is not readily available, sharable, understandable, nor usable. Human-stored knowledge is also perishiable as employees leave or retire, or simply forget.

Marvin Minsky,[2] in his ground-breaking book, *Society of Mind*, likens the human mind to an idiosyncratic and complex organization, which contains many specialists who forward and summarize their results to managers, who, in turn, report to higher levels. There is even a brain mechanism that evolved to make sense of events and provide a singular sense of self — often summarizing the environment in ways that coincide with its beliefs — that sometimes makes things up to maintain consistency. This structure is very similar to an organization's bureaucratic functions, complete with a chain of command and a public relations office to present a consistent, favorable image to the public.

An Organizational Memory may consist of many different kinds of knowledge and information:

- Directory of knowledge sources and skill sets
- Plans and schedules
- Procedures
- Principles, guidelines
- Standards, policies
- Causal models
- Process maps and workflows

- Information/data stores
- Decision rules
- Performance measures and other data
- Worked cases
- Designs of business system components
- Stakeholder and customer profiles: needs, values, expectations, perceptions
- Products and services: features, functionality, pricing, sales, repair
- Domain workforce profiles: knowledge, experience, preferences, interests
- Domain best practices
- Current state assessments and learnings

What is most important for this Store stage of KM is how the knowledge is organized and represented. Later we will discuss the Knowledge Hierarchy, various Knowledge Structures to represent knowledge, and the Knowledge Repository — an integrated storage facility.

Creating an Organizational Memory

Remember from Chapter 6 that information, knowledge, and expertise should be categorized into domains. In this regard, the organizational memory is a collection of specialized disciplines that form a network that enhances performance when applied to complex processes.

However, the organizational memory can also be viewed as a collection of many different components within an organization. One perspective is that the storage facility is composed of brains, paper, and computers. For example, individuals retain knowledge in their own memory stores, belief structures, mental models, assumptions, values, beliefs, as well as in paper and electronic files.

From another viewpoint, Walsh and Ungson[1] believe that there are six components to an organizational memory:

- Individuals (their memories and abilities)
- Culture (beliefs, values, symbols, and stories)
- Transformations (procedures and systems)
- Structures (roles and organizations)
- Ecology (facilities and ergonomics)
- External Archives (customers, competitors, industry groups, government)

However, this viewpoint ignores the vast bodies of formal knowledge that are available both within and external to the organization, not to mention knowledge available on the Internet.

Business Model

From his work in business reengineering, Beckman[3] has developed a comprehensive business model that consists of an organization and the environment in which it exists. This model describes how an organization works and interacts with its environment. The business system is defined in terms of its constituent components or dimensions, and their linkages, interactions, and feedback. In this model, processes enabled by infrastructure components create desirable products and services that meet customer needs.

This business system has two complementary perspectives: the internal organization and the external environment. The internal perspective is concerned with redesigning the process and enabling infrastructure components in order to achieve superior organizational performance. The organizational components are:

- Product/Service
- Expertise
- Process
- Management
- Workforce
- Technology

The external perspective, on the other hand, is focused on redesigning the products and services, as well as redefining and influencing the other environmental components in order to achieve greatly improved customer value and marketplace success. The environmental components are:

- Customer
- Product/Service
- Market
- Environment

Note that the Product/Service component appears twice because of differing offerings by the organization and orther market competitors.

Environmental Components

A more detailed look at the environmental components show the following attributes:

- Customer:
  —Customer profile, market segment
  —Customer needs, values, perceptions, and expectations
  —Competition, market, and industry
  —External environment: demographics, social, political, regulatory
- Product:
  —Product and service features: functionality, quality, time, and cost
  —Service process: product information, transaction, delivery, use, and repair
  —Cost, pricing, marketing, and sales
- Market:
  —Market outlook: growth, stability, decline
  —Competitive intelligence
  —Industry standards
  —Industry best practices
- Environment:
  —Demographics
  —Regulatory influences
  —Trends and drivers

Organizational Components

Organizational performance is largely dependent on processes which in turn are dependent on the infrastructure. Jointly, the infrastructure components and the processes determine the level and sustainability of organizational performance in the face of trends in customer needs, the marketplace, competition, and government regulation. The organizational components are:

- Product:
  —Product and service features: functionality, quality, time, and cost
  —Service process: product information, transaction, delivery, use, and repair
  —Cost, pricing, marketing, and sales

- Expertise:
  —Data, information, knowledge, expertise, organizational competence
  —Knowledge acquisition and management
  —Exploring, experimenting, learning, innovation, teaching
  —Centers of expertise
- Process:
  —Workflow decomposition, mapping, measures
  —Activity triggers, suppliers, resources, outcomes and interfaces
  —Policy, practices, procedures, methods
  —Workflow analysis and simulation: capacity, bottlenecks, constraints
- Management:
  —Strategic planning: mission, vision, goals, objectives, and strategies
  —Performance management and workflow optimization — scheduling, assigning, structuring, monitoring, and controlling
  —Resource: planning, budgeting, logistics, optimization, and sourcing
  —Structure: organizational, team, job, role
  —Reward: measurement, appraisal, & compensation
  —Improvement: continuous, incremental, reengineering, change
- Workforce:
  —Motivation, development, empowerment
  —Staffing and career paths
  —Culture: values, beliefs, norms, symbols, unions
- Technology:
  —IT platform and client/server architecture
  —ES: Knowledge repositories, performance support systems, personal assistants
  —Communications and groupware software

Knowledge Representation: Knowledge Structures and Inference Engines

Minsky[4] believes that the mind employs many approaches to thinking and thus to representing and organizing differing kinds of knowledge. He argues persuasively that there is no Holy Grail; no single representation that is best for all types of knowledge domains. Minsky discusses two extreme representations:

connectionist and symbolic, and explains that neither is adequate to support the sorts of intellectual performances we take for granted even in young children.

Before knowledge can be stored, it must be formally represented and organized. There are two basic dimensions to knowledge that must be represented: knowledge structures and reasoning mechanisms. Knowledge structures are passive: they organize and store the knowledge into predetermined structures. Reasoning mechanisms are active: they manipulate the structures to produce useful outputs such as inferences and answers. Each knowledge structure has its own specialized reasoning mechanism attached to it. For example, relational databases, as a form of knowledge structure, are not very useful or valuable without the corresponding query language that enables powerful explorations of data. In another instance, hypertext links and key word search add greatly to the value of the digitized raw text. Further, casebases are simply relational database structures until similarity and induction learning mechanisms are included. Finally, a rule-base by itself cannot solve complex problem situations until an inference engine is used to apply the correct rules according to its own set of control guidelines.

According to knowledge hierarchy, the simplest knowledge structure is a datum, and it has two pieces: <attribute value>. For example, <color yellow> indicates that the color is yellow. The most common knowledge structure adds an entity or object to create a triple: <object attribute value>. This allows us to represent much more complex objects. For example, <bird color yellow> asserts that there is a bird that is yellow. If we add a simple rule, such as "If <bird color yellow>, then <bird type canary>", now we have reasoned that if a bird is yellow, then it is a canary. Note that now the bird has two attributes, "color" and "type."

Cognitive psychologists recognize five types of knowledge schema:

1. Cases
2. Rules
3. Events
4. Semantic Networks
5. Models

We will discuss knowledge structures, schema, and reasoning mechanisms more fully in Chapter 10.

Kamran Parsaye and Mark Chignell,[5] in their book *Expert Systems for Experts*, describe five elementary properties of knowledge that can be used to define and represent objects and their interactions:

1. Naming (proper nouns)
2. Describing(adjectives)
3. Organizing(categorization and possession)
4. Relating(transitive verbs and relationship nouns)
5. Constraining(conditions)

Naming provides basic meaning to symbols, as well as ensuring symbol uniqueness. Constraining consists of rules that limit allowable describing, organizing, and relating operations on objects.

The following list of knowledge representation schema will be more fully developed in Chapter 10:

- Model-Based Reasoning (MBR)
  —Object Technology
  —Frames
- Rule-Based Systems (RBS)
- Case-Based Reasoning (CBR)
- Natural Language
  —Conceptual Dependencies
  —Text Generation
- Text/Documents
- Images

Expert System Concepts

Expert Systems (ES) are computer programs created to apply domain knowledge to specific problem and decision situations. Before discussing ES, however, we must define what we mean by expertise. Following is a table of the characteristics of expertise. Of course, only world-class human experts, such as chess grandmasters and medical diagnosticians, display all these characteristics in abundance. Then the question arises, how many of these traits does an expert system exhibit? The 'X' in the Human and ES columns of the table indicates whether the typical human expert or ES displays a trait. A small 'x' indicates a partially or weakly displayed characteristic.

Human	ES	Characteristic
X	X	Use narrow domain of knowledge
X	X	Perform accurately
X	X	Perform fast
X	x	Explain result
X	x	Explain reasoning
X		Learn, adapt, perform flexibly
X	x	Solve unique and unusual cases
X	x	Reason from theoretical basic principles (Model)
X	X	Reason from heuristics (Rules)
X	X	Reason from a body of experience (Cases)
x	X	Reason under uncertainty
X		Reason from common-sense and apply general world knowledge
X		Understand limits and boundaries of own knowledge
X		Explore problem characteristics early in solution process
X		Monitor skills and self-knowledge

In order to identify potential ES applications, it is useful to distinguish between the types of ES. Very often, employing one or more types of ES may be a better choice depending on several factors — the situation particulars, degree of structure in the domain knowledge, the knowledge representation schema, and user characteristics. There are three general types of ES:

1. Case-Based Reasoning (CBR)
2. Rule-Based Systems (RBS)
3. Model-Based Reasoning (MBR)

Case-Based Reasoning captures knowledge directly from experience. CBR relies on expertise in the form of worked cases. CBR works by measuring how similar a new situation is to an existing case in the case-base, and retrieving the most similar (most relevant) case. A case consists of the attributes and values of a problem situation, as well as its solution.

Rule-Based Systems (RBS)

RBS use many small slivers of knowledge organized into conditional if-then rules. Rules often represent heuristics — shortcuts or rules-of-thumb for solving problems. Rules of thumb are abstracted and generalized from experience into small chunks of knowledge. Often cases can be transformed into rules by applying Machine Learning induction techniques, thus providing more value through generalized applicability. RBS require Inference Engines to manage their reasoning process by deciding which rule to fire next when several have been triggered.

Model-Based Reasoning (MBR)

MBR provides a representational and conceptual framework for knowledge that defines both knowledge structures and inferencing methods. MBR defines and structures relevant domain objects/concepts, their attributes, and their behaviors in order to organize and control work in complex domains and perform simulations. MBR also can define the relationships between objects in terms of class hierarchies, composition, and causation. MBR can encompass, represent, and organize all types of knowledge, including CBR and RBS, as well as databases, text, images, and other media. MBR requires a well-structured, well-understood domain theory. MBR is very useful for organizing and structuring complex business domains and work processes.

Knowledge Repository

A Knowledge Repository is an on-line, computer-based storehouse of expertise, knowledge, experience, and documentation about a particular domain of expertise. A *Knowledge Domain* is defined as a specific field of study, subject area, discipline, or skill. Before a Knowledge Repository can be created, domain knowledge must be collected or elicited from experts and then be formalized so that it can be represented digitally. The Business Model described above provides a convenient way to organize business knowledge into domains. In creating a Knowledge Repository, knowledge is collected, summarized, organized, and integrated across information sources.

As we shall discuss in Chapter 11, Knowledge Repositories rely on human experts working in Centers of Expertise for their creation, development, and maintenance. In turn, these Repositories serve as the foundations and knowledge sources for the Integrated Performance Support Systems that we will cover in Chapter 10. Also in Chapter 10, we will describe the detailed workings of Knowledge Repositories.

A Knowledge Repository may consist of many different kinds of knowledge structures:

- Dictionary: Definition of terms in knowledge domain; concepts and vocabulary
- Image-Base: Digitized Images and Video
- Text-Base: Books, periodicals, manuals, handbooks, news feeds
- Document-Base: Hypertext, Form Templates
- Data-Base: Relational, Network, Hierarchical
- Case-Base: Experience as worked prototypical examples for decision-making and problem-solving
- Rule-Base: Heuristics, Decision-making, Problem-solving, Definitional Knowledge
- Script-Base: Events, Stereotypical Behavior, Procedures
- Object-Base: Concepts, Entities, Objects
- Process-Base: Process Maps
- Model-Base: Causal Models, Framework for Business System

To create a Knowledge Repository, begin with the documentation that is readily available internal to the organization. This may include work documents from business reengineering and process improvement efforts, as well as performance measurement system results. Some of these documents are especially useful:

- Stakeholder analysis
- Customer needs analysis
- Information/data stores
- Process maps and workflows
- Procedures, guidelines, and policies
- Measures and performance data from rollout
- Assessment and learnings from rollout
- Appraisal and compensation plans

Creating Casebases

Any changes to the business system, or any experiments, will result in updating the documentation in the Knowledge Repository. In addition to maintaining its currency, you will want to create at least two additional types of knowledge:

- Casebase of worked cases
- Criteria for decision-making

The Casebase represents the documentation of your experiences — your best performance, mistakes, and lessons learned. You first must determine which factors are relevant in working a case in order to arrive at the best or desired result. Next, capture the values associated with those factors; if unknown, indicate that. Once done, describe the solution process in a structured way — map sequences of tasks and decision points using a process modelling tool, if available. Finally, attach an explanation and justification for the solution. Create a separate case for each type of work, for prototypical cases, and for unusual cases.

The goal is to have broad coverage of the domain and provide instructional value. Worked cases also can be easily shared across peer work groups. The workforce can receive training through using the cases with fast updates for new types of work that employees may encounter. In addition, workers are encouraged to work through cases on their own. The cases can also be used as part of a test base for certifying the knowledge and expertise of the workforce.

Creating Rulebases

Decision-making is the second type of knowledge in which you will want to develop expertise. Poor decisions can undo much of your other efforts towards performance excellence. In the first step, you must identify all the major decisions that affect your business system. Many of these decisions will involve the management of processes. Often information or data outside the individual's knowledge is needed to make or improve the quality of the decision. As in the Casebase, identify the variables, information, and data needed to make or improve the decision.

Using Knowledge Elicitation techniques that will be discussed in Chapter 9, work with the best domain experts available to create rules that will result in good decisions. Then create cases or apply the casebase to test those rules to ensure that they work well in most situations. Rule-Based Expert System software does exist to assist in automating these knowledge sources. Two other approaches for very important, complex decisions aare to use either the Causal Flow Analysis technique or the Decision Analysis technique.

Creating Process-Bases

Process-bases are on-line maps and models of how the work in your organization gets done. Processes are usually decomposable down to the individual task level, not that you should necessarily want to go this far. We believe that the benefits from detailed Activity-Based Costing modeling are greatly overestimated when the effort required to create and retain the activity maps is factored in. The most value from process-bases results from their use in simulation and forecasting.

Creating Best Practice Knowledge Bases

Capturing knowledge about best practices requires capturing information about each component of the business system, and possibly how the components interact. This knowledge can be represented using a casebase within an object framework. Even process characteristics can be represented using an object model to simulate the process' operation.

Suggested Readings

Minsky, M. *The Society of Mind*. Simon & Schuster. 1987.
Parsaye, K. and Chignell, M. *Expert Systems for Experts*. John Wiley & Sons. 1988.

References

1. Walsh, J. and Ungson, G. "Organizational Memory." *Academy of Management Review*. 1991, Vol. 16. No. 1.
2. Minsky, M. *The Society of Mind*. Simon & Schuster. 1987.
3. Beckman, T. "Expert System Applications: Designing Innovative Business Systems through Reengineering." *Handbook of Applied Expert Systems*. Liebowitz, J., ed. CRC Press. 1998.
4. Minsky, M. "Logical vs. Analogical or Symbolic vs. Connectionist or Neat vs. Scruffy." *Artificial Intelligence at MIT, Expanding Frontiers, Volume 1*. Winston, P. ed. MIT Press. 1990.

5. Parsaye, K. and Chignell, M. *Expert Systems for Experts*. John Wiley & Sons. 1988.
6. van Heijst, G., van der Spek, R., and Kruizinga, E. "Organizing Corporate Memories." University of Amsterdam, *Social Science Informatics*. 1996.
7. Beckman, T. *Designing Innovative Business Systems through Reengineering*. Tutorial at the 4th World Congress on Expert Systems, Mexico City, 1998.

8 Sharing and Applying Knowledge: Access, Distribution, Education, and Performance

Knowledge is the beginning of practice; doing is the completion of knowing.

— Wang Yang-Ming
1498

Introduction

It should be apparent, but worth restating, that without considerable effort in capturing organizing, and storing knowledge, there will be little formal knowledge of value to access, distribute, share, and use. Of the three media in which knowledge can be stored, only the electronic form can provide significant value to the enterprise through its relative speed, simultaneous availability, and ease of access to and organization of the knowledge. Unfortunately, it is also the medium that costs the most to develop and maintain. As a short-term measure, the other two forms of storage, human minds and paper, can provide limited benefits through better design and organization of the content knowledge on paper, and use of knowledge directories that can point to sources of employee and organizational expertise and knowledge. For a discussion of electronic memories and usage, see the sections on Knowledge Repositories and Performance Support Systems in Chapter 10.

This chapter covers several aspects of knowledge sharing. The fifth stage in the knowledge management process, *Share*, first deals with individual ease of accessing and retrieving stored knowledge. This also includes navigating through Knowledge Repositories, the details of which will be discussed in Chapter 10. A more interesting and valuable concept is the proactive distribution of knowledge to interested parties or "subscribers." Both of the authors have made a life-long practice of sharing knowledge with colleagues that they believed might be of interest or value. In the Knowledge Organization, all employees should have identified subject areas of responsibility, expertise, and interest, and all employees are encouraged/expected to proactively share knowledge that may aid or impact on their colleagues.

The second aspect of the Share stage deals with communicating, collaborating, and sharing ideas, opinions, experience, and knowledge between individuals, teams, and organizational units. This aspect of knowledge sharing can be greatly facilitated through the use of such technology as telephones, fax, voice-mail, e-mail, groupware, and audio, video, and computer conferencing.

The second part of this chapter describes how knowledge is applied in performing and managing work. The sixth stage, *Apply*, covers active support for decision-making, problem-solving, performing, and managing work, as well as education and training, and job aids and tools. With the advent of Integrated Performance Support Systems (IPSS),[2] tasks can either be automated or supported/enabled through eduction, training, tools, on-line help, directories of expertise, textbases, casebases, rulebases, and modelbases. The technical aspects of IPSS will be discussed in Chapter 10.

The *Share* stage retrieves knowledge from the corporate memory and makes it accessible to users. The workforce makes their needs and personal interests known to the corporate memory which then automatically distributes any incoming new knowledge to its "subscribers" either electronically or by paper. In addition, individuals, teams, and departments often exchange ideas, opinions, gossip, knowledge, and expertise in meetings held in person or through groupware in virtual teams. It is crucial that the potentially valuable portions of these communications, discussions, arguments, and collaborations are made available to the *Capture* stage of the Knowledge Management process. For example, differing points of view and their rationales should be captured as part of any decision-making process, as well as the method used to reach the final decision.

The *Apply* stage retrieves and uses the needed knowledge in performing tasks, solving problems, making decisions, researching ideas, and learning. In order to easily access, retrieve, and apply the right pieces of knowledge, at the right prices, at the right time, in the right form, more than a query language is needed. Integrated Performance Support Systems (IPSS)[2] are being used by leading organizations to greatly increase the performance and capabilities of knowledge workers. First, to ease access, natural classification and navigation systems need to be built for browsing or retrieving knowledge. To retrieve just the right knowledge content requires that the system understand the user's purpose, context, and proficiency. To receive the knowledge at the right time requires a proactive system that monitors the user's actions and determines when it is appropriate to intervene with help in the form of a job aid or training module. Users can also customize the format in which knowledge and assistance are presented. Finally, users can access reference, advisory, testing, and certification modules.

Stage 5 — Share

In 1994, a survey was conducted by the The Knowledge Management Network founded by Rob van der Spek and Robert de Hoog[3] among 80 Dutch companies, as previously mentioned in earlier chapters. The results of this survey were quite shocking — they uncovered three bottlenecks that prevent firms from successfully applying knowledge:

- 80% of the respondents reported that there were critical business processes in which knowledge was only available to one or two persons.
- 57% of the respondents reported costly mistakes because knowledge was not available at the place and/or the point-in-time when needed.
- 52% of the respondents reported difficulties in securing knowledge when persons were transferred or when business processes were restructured.

Access and Retrieval

As discussed in Chapter 7, knowledge can be stored in several forms: in the minds of employees, on paper, on video, on audio, or electronically. Formal knowledge can be widely and immediately accessed and retrieved only by computer. Often formal knowledge in paper form can be located only with difficulty. And then to share the knowledge there are further delays due to copying and distribution. Personal mental knowledge cannot be easily accessed or retrieved by the organization. Human sources of expertise can be located through knowledge directories or personal referrals. And even then domain experts must be available in order to be queried by another employee. In light of these difficulties, it is of the greatest importance and value to first formalize and organize as much knowledge as possible and then to capture that knowledge electronically. Video, audio, and other electronic knowledge forms can be combined into multi-media forms to produce more effective presentations of knowledge. IT is critical to enabling large-scale sharing of knowledge, making it available anywhere, any time, and in any form.

However, because few organizations currently possess on-line Knowledge Repositories, they must rely primarily on more primitive methods of distributing formalized knowledge by paper, e-mail, video, and voice-mail. Efficient indexing of paper-based knowledge is critical for retrieval. Without a computer network, organizations must rely on fax, express mail, and interoffice mail, depending on the required speed of retrieval.

Reference Knowledge and Knowledge Directories

In Chapters 5 and 6, we described how to assess current knowledge, skills, expertise, and experience, and in Chapter 7 we discussed how to create knowledge resources and directories. This knowledge assessment forms part of every employee's profile, and is readily available to any employee. In addition, we suggested that knowledge or expertise directories, as well as those for interests, be created for each domain and made available to all employees.

Domain experts are valuable commodities. Their time shouldn't be wasted in answering routine questions. We believe that automated, online assistance should be provided for routine problems and questions. In fact, as it matured, the discipline of knowledge engineering found that the big gains in overall productivity came from capturing and distributing routine knowledge and expertise from domain experts. Expert systems then either perform the work directly or are available as assistants to support novices and less proficient performers. Rather than stealing the expert's source of value to the company, in most situations the expert systems freed up the time of domain experts to deal with truly difficult and complex issues, problems, and decisions. We believe that other important roles of domain experts are to act as researchers, educators and knowledge builders and evaluators.

Distribution of Knowledge — Knowledge Interests

In addition to providing access to human, paper, and electronic sources of knowledge, knowledge usage should also include automatic distribution of knowledge to interested parties — individual employees, organizational units, and even electronic entities. Van Heijst, van der Spek, and Kruizinga of the University of Amsterdam[1] suggest that corporate memories need a facility for deciding who should be informed about a particular new piece of knowledge. Manual distribution lists by knowledge domain could serve this function until electronic means are available. However, eventually systems should keep records so that the same information is not distributed twice.

Ideally, notification and content would be delivered electronically to requestors. Several researchers, such as Thomas Malone, Barbara Grosz, and others, have suggested that intelligent electronic agents would search the Intranet and Internet for knowledge of interest to employees, departments, or other electronic agents. As intelligent agents, the "found" knowledge then might be subjected to screening before being presented to the requestor.

Collaborate across Functions

Collaboration is the sharing of ideas, opinions, and perspectives between knowledgeable people with differing backgrounds. One of the principles of organizational learning is to incorporate a variety of perspectives in any work performed. These perspectives can be across work groups, specialities, functions, and even external to the organization. Internal perspectives might be the upstream and downstream processes from your own, business improvement and management consultants, and individuals and functions with knowledge or expertise in the domains of interest. External perspectives might include customers and stakeholders, regulatory agencies, and academia/industry special interest groups in the areas of expertise.

Sharing Domain Knowledge across the Organization/Knowledge Sharing Conferences

Employees with expertise and experience should be periodically debriefed in order to capture and share their valuable knowledge. One way of doing this is through periodic domain conferences.

Establish a network of peer working groups within your areas of expertise. This network should hold a conference once or twice a year to discuss problems, issues, and ideas within their domain specialty. Separate conferences should be held for process groups.

Stage 6 — Apply

The sixth stage of the KM process, Apply, is the flip side of the Share stage. For the KM process to be effective, not only must knowledge be readily available and shared, but also the recipient of that knowledge must make good use of it — apply it to real work situations. Only in this way will the knowledge attain its maximum value to the organization.

Knowledge can be applied directly by a person or computer to perform work, or indirectly as a job aid or tool to support the performance of that work. It can also be used to manage the work through work classification, scheduling, assignment, monitoring, and evaluation. Finally, knowledge can be applied even more indirectly to improve understanding and subsequent performance, flexibility, and adaptability through the education and training of the workforce.

Factors in Performance

Acquiring and Serving Customers

Acquiring new customers and serving existing ones is a critical capability for every organization. Beckman[5] has sketched out what a Knowledge Repository in the customer knowledge domain might look like. This Customer Repository would create customer profiles, capture and store historical information on customers, capture and structure new information from customers, solicit and capture customer feedback, identify potential new customers, and link this knowledge to related Repositories such as those for Sales, Marketing, Product, and Service. For example, such a Customer Repository might have the following categories and attributes:

- Company Data (Name, Location, Industry, Gross Revenue)
- Company Contact (Name, Address, Phone, E-mail)
- Needs (Preferences, Expectations, Values, Interests)
- Prior Purchases (Product, Service, Date, Amount)
- Transaction Data for Each Purchase (Sales Terms, Financing Terms, Payment History, Delivery/Installation Timeliness, Service Contracts)
- Customer Service History (Requests, Repairs, Information, Training)
- Customer Feedback (Complaints, Compliments, Suggestions, Ideas)

The Customer Repository, in conjunction with the Product and Service Repositories, and the Sales and Marketing Repositories, would be readily available to the salesforce. Such knowledge could easily give your sales and marketing departments an edge over the competition. Based on information and knowledge in these Repositories, an online expert system could prompt the salesforce to suggest related product lines that might be of interest to the customer.

Educate, Coach, and Consult with Workforce

Clearly, it is important to distribute problems, issues, knowledge, and learnings quickly and efficiently throughout the organization. Without electronic support, when employees need help or advice, they must take the initiative to locate and contact knowledgeable peers. A likely resource will be to reference the recently created directories of personal and organizational expertise that can locate domain experts and practitioners who can provide needed training, assistance, and coaching.

Online training, coaching, and consulting require that both the needed Knowledge Repositories and Integrated Performance Support Systems (IPSS)[2] be established. IPSS can even proactively assist the workforce in improving their expertise and performance. However, domain experts are the ultimate resource — they must build and enhance the Knowledge Repositories and related IPSS, as well as support the workforce's knowledge and performance through formal education and training, consulting services, and spot coaching.

As will be covered in more detail in Chapter 10, IPSS can provide instructional services on a continuum from context-sensitive help and job aids to tutoring, training, and advice. Expanding on Winslow and Bramer[2], we suggest that there are several types of services that can be supplied to the workforce:

- Work profile
- Advisory
- Training
- Job Aids and Help
- Information
- Evaluation/Certification
- Reference
- Human Resources
- Performance Measures: Organizational, Group, and Personal

Business Reengineering — Improving Performance

In addition to production work, many organizations will periodically initiate development projects. Development projects reflect larger-scale changes that could not be realistically made immediately to the production or customer service process being changed. Therefore, these improvement efforts are taken off-line to be designed and developed by domain experts, senior practitioners, customers, and stakeholders in the subject knowledge domains that are relevant to the overall project. Often these projects may bring together participants from five to ten knowledge domains.

Business reengineering is considered the largest scale, most broadly scoped, and most radical form of improvement or development initiative. Business reengineering is of similar age to KM — it was formally christened by Michael Hammer in 1990. Reengineering grew out of the quality movement, but it also has roots in work systems design, process innovation, and leading practices from management consulting firms. According to Hammer (Hammer and Champy, 1993), "Reengineering is the fundamental rethinking and radical redesign of business processes to achieve dramatic improvements in critical measures of performance." Beckman[6] proposes a more results-focused definition: "Reengineering is the fundamental rethinking and radical redesign of an entire business system to achieve dramatic improvements in customer value and organizational performance."

- Fundamental rethinking starts fresh by examining the mission and strategy, scanning the environment, as well as surfacing and challenging existing assumptions and policies — not just accepting the existing situation.
- Radical redesign starts with best practices and then applies innovative information technology (IT) — not just improving incrementally.
- Business system means multiple components are redesigned, including products, services, management, IT, and motivation — not just reworking the process.
- Dramatic improvements are in both customer value and organizational performance. Innovative new products and services or features are created. Performance gains are at least 50% in measures such as functionality, cost, quality, and time — not just 10-20% gains in internal measures of performance.

The primary focus of reengineering should be external — on customer value expressed through products and services. The secondary emphasis should be internal — on organizational performance organized around the work processes.

Reengineering Methodology

A methodology is a body of methods, rules, and postulates employed by a discipline. Most methodologies consist of three parts:

1. Purpose or goal state
2. Model or system with components, features, or dimensions
3. Process that achieves the purpose

Reengineering methodologies are basically formal design processes. For reengineering, the goal is creating a highly desirable or ideal business system that delivers greatly improved organizational performance and/or customer value. The design artifact is the business system that is divided into components, each one representing a different aspect or functionality. Finally, the design process is the reengineering life cycle, beginning with project definition and scoping, and ending with implementation.

A good methodology provides guidance and structure without being overly restrictive. It should also strike a balance between theory and practice. Methodologies should be thorough and disciplined without being too detailed and inflexible. Methodologies should occupy a middle ground between intuition and a cookbook. Some ideas are to provide principles, guidelines, and assessment tools, as well as examples, tips, and pitfalls.

Reengineering Life Cycle

The Reengineering Life Cycle is the content and sequence of the methodology. The Life Cycle describes in detail how the future Business System will be defined, developed, and implemented. The methodology spans business activities from strategic planning, through product development and process redesign, to operations. The author's version of the methodology has five phases (Beckman, 1996):

Phase 1 — Determine Strategy
Phase 2 — Assess Current State
Phase 3 — Develop Conceptual Design
Phase 4 — Build and Test Detailed Design
Phase 5 — Implement Design

The *Determine Strategy* phase focuses on setting and/or validating the strategic direction through analysis of industry, market segments, customer needs, competition, core competencies, and external trends and forces. Mission, vision, improvement initiatives, and plans are melded into a business strategy. Then strategic initiatives, primarily reengineering projects, are scoped and aligned to ensure commitment of executive leadership. Outcomes from Phase 1 are the business strategy, targeted market segments, and approved project charter.

The *Assess Current State* phase assesses the current state of each of the components in the Business System. Needs, values, and expectations of current customers, targeted market segments, including the interests and issues of key stakeholders, are determined, clustered, and prioritized. Next, constraints such as project funding, political sacred cows, technology feasibility, market dynamics, resources, and workforce expertise are determined. Conflicting needs and unnecessary constraints are negotiated and resolved. The resultant customer needs then are transformed into high-level business requirements and constraints. Further, problems and defects in the current system are identified and also converted into requirements. The outcomes from Phase 2 are the case for action that documents the current state, defined value and performance gaps, and a set of high-level business requirements and constraints.

The *Develop Conceptual Design* phase starts with the high-level business requirements and tries to design an ideal system by decomposing the design into work system components. Design enablers such as customer needs, value gaps, performance gaps, best practices, innovative IT, and creative thinking are used to improve and enhance the design. Next, design functionality/features are prioritized by the stakeholders, clustered into releases, and assessed for costs, benefits, risks, and dependencies. Outcomes are the conceptual design and high-level business case.

The *Build and Test Detailed Design* phase takes the conceptual design and decomposes each component into its detailed attributes. An operational prototype of each component is developed and tested for feasibility and effectiveness. After component testing, an integrated test is conducted of the overall design that is evaluated by the various customers and stakeholders.

Design modifications are made and tested until the customers are satisfied. Outcomes are the detailed design, release strategy, and business case. The *Implement* phase first conducts a release pilot at an operational site to field test the design. Once proven, releases are rolled out across all sites. The final activity, Transition to Operate, includes measurement, problem solving, and learning.

At the end of each phase, a decision point with three options — go, no go, or wait — is used to determine whether staffing and funding resources for the next phase will be approved and committed. Thus, resources are both managed efficiently, and more promising or urgent initiatives may displace or delay, but not kill, an existing one.

Suggested Readings

Birchall, D. and Lyons, L. *Creating Tomorrow's Organization: Unlocking the Benefits of Future Work.* Pitman Publishing. 1995.

Carr, C. Smart Training: *The Manager's Guide to Training for Improved Performance.* McGraw–Hill. 1992.

Chawla, S. and Renesch, J., ed. *Learning Organizations: Developing Cultures for Tomorrow's Workplace.* Productivity Press. 1995.

Gery, G. *Electronic Performance Support Systems: How and Why to Remake the Workplace through the Strategic Application of Technology.* Gery Perf. Press. 1991.

Leonard-Barton, D. *Wellsprings of Knowledge: Building and Sustaining the Sources of Innovation.* Harvard Business School Press. 1995.

Mabey, C. and Iles, P., ed. *Managing Learning.* Routledge. 1994.

Marquardt, M. *Building the Learning Organization.* McGraw–Hill. 1996.

Martin, J. *The Great Transition: Using the Seven Disciplines of Enterprise Engineering to Align People, Technology, and Strategy.* AMACOM. 1995.

Tobin, D. *Transformational Learning: Renewing Your Company through Knowledge and Skills.* John Wiley. 1996.

Winslow, C. and Bramer, W. *Future Work: Putting Knowledge to Work in the Knowledge Economy.* Free Press. 1994.

References

1. van Heijst, G., van der Spek, R, and Kruizinga, E. "Organizing Corporate Memories." University of Amsterdam, *Social Science Informatics.* 1996.
2. Winslow, C. and Bramer, W. *Future Work: Putting Knowledge to Work in the Knowledge Economy.* Free Press. 1994.
3. van der Spek, R. and de Hoog, R. "Towards a Methodology for Knowledge Management." Knowledge Management Network. 1994.

4. Rifkin, G. "Buckman Labs: Nothing but Net." *Fast Company.* June–July 1996.
5. Beckman, T. *Applying AI to Business Reengineering.* 146 pages. ©1996. Presented at the Third World Congress on Expert Systems, Seoul, Korea, February 1996.
6. Beckman, T. "Expert System Applications: Designing Innovative Business Systems through Reengineering." *Handbook of Applied Expert Systems.* Liebowitz, J., ed. CRC Press, 1998.

9 Creating Knowledge

He who cannot change the very frame of his thought can never change reality.

— Anwar Sadat

The prime business of business is learning.

— Harrison Owen
The Business of Learning
1991

The reasonable man adapts himself to the world: the unreasonable one persists in trying to adapt the world to himself. Therefore, all progress depends on the unreasonable man.

— George Bernard Shaw
Man and Superman
1903

Introduction

In this chapter, we focus on the *Create* stage. The extraction and creation of new knowledge involves learning, knowledge elicitation, lessons learned, creative thinking, research, experimentation, discovery, and innovation. There are also many organizational activities that have the potential to result in the creation of new knowledge. However, far too often the learnings from these activities are not extracted, nor are they stored or disseminated to potentially interested parties. These knowledge-rich organizational activities with great potential for learning include:

- Knowledge Elicitation
- Strategic Planning
- Research
- Organizational Transformation
- Business Reengineering
- Continuous Improvement
- Environmental Monitoring
- Competitive Intelligence
- Organizational Assessment
- Operational Review
- Project Post-Implementation Review
- Customer and Stakeholder Needs, Preferences, and Requirements Analyses
- Benchmarking and Best Practices
- Measurement and Reporting Systems
- Decision Making
- Problem Solving
- Lessons Learned

You might question whether there is any real difference between collecting existing knowledge and creating and extracting new knowledge. And what about an organization that learns new knowledge of either kind? After all, even if an organization is simply ignorant of some generally well-known and well-understood knowledge, and then becomes aware of it by chance or by intentional search, it is still new knowledge to that organization that must be absorbed and learned.

Ikujiro Nonaka[2] feels that we should think of businesses as "knowledge-creating companies." He believes that there are four basic patterns for creating knowledge in any organization:

- From tacit to tacit — apprenticing to learn the master's skills
- From explicit to explicit — taking existing formal knowledge and transforming it

- From tacit to explicit — creating new formal knowledge that can be used directly by others
- From explicit to tacit — internalizing a new idea, gaining an understanding or skill

Learning

In general, learning is the acquisition and application of new knowledge, skills, and experiences that change behavior, thought, and beliefs to improve performance, or to better adapt to or to take advantage of the environment. D. Kolb[8] has proposed a learning cycle that is comprised of four steps:

Step 1 — Concrete experience
Step 2 — Observation and reflection leading to:
Step 3 — The formulation of concepts and generalizations resulting in:
Step 4 — The development of hypotheses which are to be tested in future action, leading in turn to new experiences

In this model, according to Birchall and Lyons[5], in addition to knowledge and understanding, the learner also undergoes changes in attitude and develops the vital skills of learning how to learn. During this discussion of learning, we will draw heavily on the work of Birchall and Lyons, Garvin, Marquardt, and Martin.

A. Jahshapara[6] has proposed that learning can occur at three levels in an organization:

1. Individual
2. Team
3. Organizational

To these three levels of learning, we add a fourth, Machine. The Knowledge Repository contains tools that can transform a lower form of knowledge into a higher form in the Knowledge Hierarchy. In the next chapter, we will describe how the AI discipline of Machine Learning can be used to automatically learn new concepts and rules, as well as to dynamically improve the performance of many types of business processes and systems. Birchall and Lyons[5] in their excellent book, *Creating Tomorrow's Organization*, expand on how IT can be applied to enable learning at the individual, team, and organizational levels.

Individual Learning

According to Michael Marquardt[7], individual learning refers to the change of skills, insights, knowledge, attitudes, and values acquired by a person through self-study, technology-based instruction, and observation. We expand that definition to include any type of instruction as well as experimentation.

Team Learning

Marquardt[7] defines team learning as the increase in knowledge, skills, and competencies that are accomplished by and within groups. James Martin[9] believes that there is great power in learning that occurs during the teamwork in serving customers through a "value stream." His value stream is an end-to-end process where customer needs are the inputs and desired products and services are the outcomes. Most team learning focuses on process analysis and continuous improvement.

Organizational Learning

David Garvin[1] has described the learning organization as "an organization skilled at creating, acquiring, and transferring knowledge, and at modifying its behavior to reflect new knowledge and insights." Marquardt[7] builds on this definition by stating that a learning organization "is continually transforming itself to better manage and use knowledge for corporate success; it empowers people within and outside the organization to learn as they work, and it utilizes technology to maximize learning and production."

Developing organizational learning and expertise is one of the most important activities for long-term organizational performance improvement and flexibility. It is not enough for individuals to learn. Unless those learnings are distributed and incorporated into the daily workplace, much of the potential value is lost. Organizational learning means that a common language, understanding, and integration of broad concepts such as processes, management, and expertise have occurred. That is, the majority of the workforce and managers in an organization can readily converse about technical, process, and managerial issues. And the organization will collectively modify its behavior in light of the new knowledge. The general idea is that intentional, structured organizational learning will improve workforce and managerial expertise, and that this expertise will inevitably lead to superior performance and more new learnings.

According to Daniel Garvin[1] of the Harvard Business School, effective learning organizations are skilled at five main activities:

1. Problem-solving
2. Experimenting with new ideas
3. Learning from mistakes
4. Learning from the success of others — best practices
5. Transferring knowledge quickly and effectively throughout the organization

Marquardt and Reynolds believe that organizational learning occurs through the following activities:[3]

- Collaborate Across Functions
- Encourage Exploration and Experimentation
- Identify Best Practices
- Update Organizational Memory with New Learnings

Collaborating across functions was covered in Chapter 8.

Sources of Learning

Now we will examine some of the most valuable sources for creating new knowledge. We will describe the following learning sources in some detail.

- Self-learning
- Learning from Experts
- Learning from Customers
- Learning from the Competition
- Learning from the Environment
- Learning from Industry
- Learning from Experimentation
- Learning from Creative Thinking

Extracting Lessons Learned: Self-Learning

Lessons learned are a valuable potential by-product of a work activity. These learnings require conscious and reflective review and evaluation by observers, participants, customers, and stakeholders. Business improvement activities such as business reengineering, process improvement, and organizational transformation can provide a wealth of feedback. This feedback would then be used to improve the methodology, training, and their implementation — a kind of incremental improvement. In addition, operational reviews, post-implementation project reviews, and performance appraisals can all be valuable sources of lessons learned.

Lessons Learned

Development initiatives, project teams, task forces, quality improvement teams, and other improvement efforts should be debriefed immediately at the end of, and also during longer-term development efforts. Much can be learned about problems and issues with methods, techniques, tools, technologies, and procedures that can be reused and transferred to other projects. In addition, the perspectives, skill sets, and related training needed by the teams can be better understood and improved on. Further, the quality of the change and project management, as well as the alignment and integration with strategic direction can be assessed for future management development needs. Finally, the project development life cycle can be examined for weaknesses in scoping, requirements, analysis, design, building, testing, and implementation.

Knowledge Elicitation: Learning from Experts

There is a tremendous amount of intellectual capital contained in the minds of your company's domain experts and senior practitioners. We believe that it is essential to formalize this tacit expertise where possible so that it can be replicated, distributed, and taught to less proficient employees to raise their levels of performance and competence. In addition, by making this knowledge explicit, very often domain experts and senior practitioners can discuss, collaborate, and extend the body of expertise. Knowledge elicitation is really learning from experts.

Knowledge Elicitation, also known as knowledge acquisition, is a sub-discipline within Knowledge Engineering that is used to build Expert Systems. Knowledge Elicitation is the transfer and transformation of problem-solving expertise from a knowledge source such as a domain expert to a computer program. It focuses on the techniques that are used to extract tacit knowledge from a domain expert. Part of this process of elicitation of tacit or unconscious knowledge involves determining how the knowledge is structured. Another AI discipline known as Knowledge Representation is used to determine what the most appropriate form or Knowledge Structure is for the new pieces of knowledge. In conjunction with Knowledge Representation, these methods can be used to collect, organize, integrate, and summarize knowledge and expertise about a particular specialty/domain. Please see Chapter 7 for details on the nature of knowledge, expertise, Knowledge Representations, and the Knowledge Hierarchy.

Hayes-Roth[12] has proposed a five-stage process for Knowledge Acquisition:

1. Identification — Identify problem characteristics
2. Conceptualization — Identify concepts, attributes, relationships, and functions to represent knowledge
3. Formalization — Design structure to organize and represent knowledge
4. Implementation — Elicit detailed expertise
5. Testing — Validate expertise

A variety of techniques are used to elicit knowledge from domain experts:

- Interviews: Structured and unstructured
- Introspection: Process Tracing and Protocol Analysis
- Observation: Task Analyses
- Repertory Grid Analysis
- Conceptual Hierarchy
- Ordered Tree
- Object Analysis and Design
- Empirical Induction
- Difficult Case Method
- Generic Ontologies
- Problem-Solving Ontologies

Debriefing Domain Experts

There are several major opportunities or events that may occur when knowledge and expertise should be elicited from a domain expert or senior practitioner:

- Retirement: capture years of experience and expertise easily
- Promotion: to a non-technical job
- Downsizing/Firing: a substantial bonus should be offered here for knowledge
- New Hires: capture their expertise before they are too busy
- Consultants: get mind dumps of their expertise — insist on their teaching your staff
- Industry Conferences/Seminars: experts are often gracious about sharing their knowledge with you — pose difficult theoretical and practical problems, or hire them as consultants

Monitor And Solicit Customer Feedback: Learning from Customers

Monitoring, soliciting, and acting on customer feedback is one of the most important activities in management. However, due to the pressure of operational problems, it is often given the least time. Customer needs, values, and expectations should be reflected in the product and service features that your process provides. In addition, results measures should monitor your performance on process outcomes. Remember: the interface between your subprocess and the next downstream subprocess is a miniature version of the overall process. Therefore, that interface/outcome/handoff also is a product or service, and the downstream subprocess is your internal customer. The reason for negotiating this interface is to optimize the larger process to satisfy the end customer.

Customer feedback is extremely important — it gives you valuable information and ideas for improvement that may not have shown up in your results measures or other problem detection mechanisms. Feedback is either solicited or unsolicited, and consists of complaints, problems, and suggestions. Complaints and problems must be analyzed at both individual and system levels. It is not enough simply to resolve the individual customer's complaint or problem, you must also determine if there is a systemic problem. In any event, after feedback is logged in and analyzed, within a reasonable amount of time all customers must receive a reasoned response, even if it is an interim or negative one.

To make it easy to give unsolicited feedback, provide both downstream and end customers with telephone and fax numbers, as well as e-mail addresses. Also distribute a Feedback Log form to all customers to make it easier to analyze and act on. Actively soliciting customer opinions and ideas is also a valuable source of direction and ideas for improvement. See a marketing text for guidance on how to prepare questionnaires and implement surveys. Remember: Be sure to publicly recognize and thank those customers whose feedback resulted in improvements to the business system, and if appropriate, reward those customers for their contributions.

Competitive Intelligence: Learning from the Competition

According to Larry Kahaner,[5] "Competitive intelligence is a systemic program for gathering and analyzing information about your competitors' activities and general business trends to further your own company's goals." Competitive intelligence is environmental scanning with an edge to it. In his book, *Competitive Intelligence*, Kahaner lists the uses of a formal program for competitive intelligence:

- Support management decision-making
- Anticipate changes in the marketplace
- Anticipate actions of competitors
- Discover new or potential competitors
- Learn from the successes and failures of others
- Increase the range and quality of acquisition targets
- Learn about new technologies, products, and processes that affect your business
- Learn about political legislation, or regulatory changes that can affect your business
- Enter a new business
- Look at your own business practices with an open mind
- Help implement management improvement strategies

Kahaner equates intelligence with knowledge and therefore the above list applies to Knowledge Management as well. His process for competitive intelligence is similar to portions of our Knowledge Management process.

Environmental Scanning: Learning from the Environment

Environmental scanning is broader-scoped than competitive intelligence, and looks at trends in industries, technologies, government policies, and demographics. One of the best ways of doing scanning today is on the Internet, where there is a wealth of knowledge, information, data, noise, and garbage. The Internet search engines are getting better, and the depth and breadth of sites is also improving.

Best Practices Research: Learning from Industry

Unlike competitive intelligence, benchmarking and best practices are friendly, cooperative efforts between two enterprises. Usually direct rivals in the same business are not partners in benchmarking. Companies search out recognized leaders in processes, products, or services, and then understand, copy, and/or modify their successes to fit the organizational culture.

Why would a company share the secrets of their success? The prestige of being recognized as a global leader or best-in-class company often far outweighs the sharing of key competitive practices. Recognized leaders attract the best talent. Company share prices often reflect premium valuations, higher than others in the industry. Often, the source of the competitive advantage being benchmarked cannot be easily copied. What is important is usually more than just the process. Superior process performance rests largely on the infrastructure business system components that support and enable the process. Recall the discussion of Business System components in earlier chapters.

Begin this activity by identifying the categories of best practices you are interested in. Examine the various Business System components, paying special attention to the process, product and service, expertise, IT, and motivation components. Also examine the core competencies that were determined as part of your strategic assessment.

You may want to examine best practices both within and external to your organization. Internally, the most relevant and valuable best practices are likely to be found in the process, product and service, and customer components. Begin communications across all peer sites, and implement these best practices as deemed appropriate.

When you look externally at best practices, try to abstract the process that you are studying. For example, rather than looking only at competitors in your industry, look at more generic processes such as order fulfillment. Externally, good sources of best practices will often come from industry, academia, textbooks, journals, and the Internet. Warning: Be sure that most of the components of your business system are similar to those from which you are transferring the practices. Otherwise, the changes will most likely not achieve the desired improvement.

Update Organizational Memory with New Learnings

When employees from Japanese companies attend conferences, seminars, workshops, or training, they are required to report back on what they learned and share and discuss it with their colleagues. These could be new findings on competitors, markets, products, forecasts, or techniques. These learnings should also be categorized and added to the organizational memory.

Organizational Knowledge Assessment

In order to capture the knowledge within the organization, it is essential to perform an assessment of current knowledge, skills, expertise, and experience in the workforce. This assessment must include all employees, even executives. In addition to the individuals in the workforce, organizational and electronic capabilities should be assessed too.

It is essential to assess those knowledge domains that support the core competencies. But, it is also wise to capture these data for non-core competencies as well. It is hard to know in advance which data, information, and knowledge will come in handy tomorrow.

Innovation: Learning from Experimentation

Jim Clemmer[10] has proposed a process for innovation that he calls the "innovation funnel" that consists of four main stages:

Stage 1. Exploration: Search for strategic partnerships, unresolved problems, latent and unmet customer needs.
Stage 2. Experimentation
Stage 3. Development
Stage 4. Integration

In his model, there are many feedback loops, and the process need not even proceed stage by stage — it can sometimes even skip stages. He believes, as we do, in the concept of iterative prototyping, where an idea is progressively developed into a robust product with much customer feedback and involvement.

A Japanese model of innovation proposed by Tatsuno[4] is a wheel divided into five phases:

1. Idea search
2. Idea nurturing
3. Idea breakthroughs
4. Idea refinement
5. Idea recycling

The phase that is least practiced in the West is the notion of idea recycling, where old ideas are reconsidered to spark new concepts, or are directly reused.

According to Dorothy Leonard-Barton[11] in her excellent book, *Wellsprings of Knowledge*, management's role in supporting experimentation and prototyping is to:

1. Create a climate that tolerates and even encourages experimentation.
2. See that a lot of experimentation and prototyping actually occurs; and
3. Set in place mechanisms to ensure that the organization learns from those activities.

Clemmer[10] has also observed, "If innovation is truly important to you, you'll hire and promote unconventional thinkers, 'boat rockers,' and passionate people who have a history of successfully bucking the system."

Encourage Exploration and Experimentation

Achieving high performance is one primary objective motivating knowledge gathering and learning; innovating to create future capabilities is another. In order to innovate, one must explore and experiment in the subject domain, and across related domains. Jim Clemmer[10] believes that exploration is a broad, open search for possible opportunities:

- Strategic partnerships
- Unresolved problems

- Latent or unmet customer needs
- New products and services
- New customer segments

Human Creativity: Learning from Creative Thinking

Creative thinking can be applied in many business settings. For example, creative thinking techniques can be applied during visioning, strategic planning, product and process design, problem-solving, and decision-making. There are a very large number of techniques ranging from brainstorming to visualization to provocative operators. Techniques exist for individuals as well as groups. As discussed in the next section, creative thinking can be applied to problem definition and scoping, assessment, as well as to solution generation.

In his excellent book, *Creativity and Innovation in Information Systems Organizations*, Daniel Couger[4] explains that much of the power of creative thinking comes from consecutively applying divergent and convergent thinking to each phase of a problem-solving process. Divergent thinking is generating a wide range of ideas, expanding the field of possibilities. Convergent thinking is selecting the most promising ideas, narrowing the field of possibilities. Couger also describes guidelines for divergence and convergence:

Divergence Guidelines

- Defer judgment
- Quantity breeds quality
- Piggyback on previous ideas
- Combine and modify ideas
- Think in pictures
- Stretch for more ideas

Convergence Guidelines

- Be systematic
- Develop evaluation criteria
- Use intuition
- Challenge assumptions and surface biases

- Avoid premature convergence
- Satisfice, rather than optimize
- Use quantitative optimization techniques
- Use heuristics
- Assess risks

A Creative Problem-Solving Method

The techniques from the previous section can be put to good use in the Creative Problem-Solving (CPS) method presented here. This generic problem-solving approach can also be applied to other tasks such as decision-making, monitoring and analyzing performance, monitoring customer feedback, and developing organizational learning and knowledge. Conversely, ideas and techniques are also borrowed from these tasks.

Once the precepts of the Knowledge Organization have begun to be implemented, it is important to follow up with improvement programs for every business system component. One important way to improve any process or procedure is to quickly identify and solve problems. This CPS method is a good one for quickly obtaining substantial process improvements.

The problem-solving method presented here was greatly influenced by ideas and techniques in Daniel Couger's [4] book. There are six steps in the problem-solving process:

Step 1 — Define Problem
Step 2 — Analyze Problem
Step 3 — Generate Solution Ideas
Step 4 — Evaluate and Select Solution
Step 5 — Test and Implement Solution
Step 6 — Document and Share Results

Step 1 — Define Problem

Problem definition is about framing and scoping the problem. How we define a problem usually determines how we analyze it. Very often, too little time is spent on this step, resulting in solving the wrong problem. Another common effect of insufficient problem exploration is expending several times the effort later on to remedy problems that could have been avoided or prevented. Common mistakes to be avoided in problem definition are:

- Defining the symptom rather than the underlying problem
- Defining the problem too narrowly
- Defining the problem too broadly
- Failing to incorporate multiple perspectives
- Applying an unnecessary or invalid assumption
- Incorporating a solution into the problem definition

There are two types of problem-finding: reactive and proactive. In reactive problem-finding, the problem is obvious and urgent — it comes looking for you. Operational or process problems are often very obvious — the process stops working or downstream customers are very upset. There is a gap between the disturbed state of the system and its normal state.

In proactive problem-finding, you must select the next area for improvement. However, in the absence of the obvious and the urgent, finding the most promising opportunity to work on may take some analysis. Continuous improvement implies that there is always a new problem to be identified and solved, an area designated for improvement. Here there is a gap between the normal state of the system and the desired state.

How does one select the next problem or area for improvement from many alternatives? It may be that only by examining and/or analyzing measures data can the most significant problem area be detected. Thus, there is a natural iteration and interplay between Steps 1 and 2, and also with Tasks 2 and 3. The results of the Analyze Problem task often lead to a revision in the problem scope. Another issue is that often only the symptoms of the underlying problem have been discovered, rather than the root cause. Thus, analytical approaches are often needed to uncover the true problem.

There are several useful techniques from creative thinking that you can use to better define problems:

- Problem Restatement
- Progressive Abstraction
- Boundary Examination
- Problem Formulation

In the first technique, the problem is restated from the perspective of different stakeholders. The idea is to uncover and understand our biases by examining the problem from differing perspectives. Perform a stakeholder analysis, including customers/users, management, union, oversight, competitors, affected employees, and domain experts.

Problems are often too narrowly defined. The Progressive Abstraction technique explores the problem space by expanding the scope of the problem until a satisfactory problem definition is found. By moving through progressively higher levels of problem abstraction, the problem structure and relationships are better understood.

The Boundary Examination technique helps us to rethink our frames of reference by challenging unnecessary constraints, assumptions, rules, and policies. By suspending these various types of boundaries, we can find new ways of looking at the problem. A list of constraint types to review in the context of your problem are: physical, locational, spatial, temporal, logical, resource, human, legal, and cultural. Incorrect or unnecessary assumptions are often created based on faulty understanding of the true nature of constraints. Once an assumption is found that causes or contributes to the problem, attempt to prove the assumption false. If false, destroy the assumption, rule, or policy and redefine your problem accordingly.

The final technique is forming the problem statement itself. A well-stated problem has four components:

1. Invitational Stem
2. Ownership
3. Action
4. Goal

For example, "In what ways might (stem) we (owner) improve (action) the information provided to Finance to improve their decision-making (goal)?" In addition, it pays to keep the problem statement as simple as possible, in an active voice, and positive.

Step 2 — Analyze Problem

How well we analyze a problem strongly determines whether we find a solution and the solution's quality. Problem analysis requires that we decompose the problem into its constituent parts or its relevant factors. If we have a good model of the problem domain, then we have already defined the objects and their related attributes and values, as well as their behaviors. Products tend to focus on attributes and values and relationships between objects; processes tend to focus on behaviors of objects. Even if we do not have a good model of the problem domain, we may know how to fix many problems based on their symptoms/factors. The existence and absence of certain symptoms, and their values often allow us to prescribe specific repairs or treatments to solve the problem.

Each of the following recommended approaches uses certain types of objects or factors and their related attributes and values to characterize, structure, and analyze a problem. Depending on the type of problem and the information available to you, we suggest that you choose one (or more) of the following approaches:

- Performance metrics
- Business system components
- Barriers to high performance
- Causal analysis

The first approach categorizes the problem according to performance metrics. For example, by analyzing process measures at selected levels of decomposition, the problem area often can be isolated. If there is a timeliness problem, look for bottlenecks — those activities that consume far more cycle time than others at the same level, or have very low actual to elapsed time ratios. Similarly, if process costs are too high, use Activity-Based Costing to find those activities that consume far more resources than others at the same level, or have very low value-added ratios. Analyzing quality problems is somewhat more complicated. The root cause of unacceptably poor quality measures must be determined. One method is to locate activities from which the most rejects and reworks originate. Additional measures may have to be added temporarily in order to determine the source of poor quality.

The second approach categorizes which components of the business system are implicated in the problem. Gap analyses attemp to find value gaps (the customer is not satisfied) and performance gaps (the process or tis supporting components are broken). One method of doing this is to compare the existing component assessment with best practices for that component and see where there are large differences.

Many process problems can be identified using the first approach. However, conformance to redesigned policies, processes, rules, and procedures must be confirmed. If these are not being followed, the reason must be determined and acted on. For example, if the measurement, appraisal, and compensation systems do not reward conformance, and in fact discourage conformance, then changes must be made to these systems to bring them into alignment with the purpose and goals of the business system and the management methods suggested in this activity. Reeducation and redesigned reward systems for both managers and workers may be needed to change old behaviors that are no longer appropriate. If the existing IS does not support user needs, then expensive manual workarounds may be used to circumvent the IS. Skill deficiencies or lack of up-to-date information in the workforce can often result in poor quality and excessive costs. Coaching, training, or reassignment may be indicated to solve deficiencies in expertise. Lack of up-to-date information usually means a breakdown in communications by management to the workforce. Lack of motivation to use the new system can result from cultural norms at odds with the redesigned system. Most of the remedies mentioned above must be consistently applied over time to effect change in the organization's underlying values and beliefs.

A third approach looks at the factors that comprise performance. There are five factors that contribute to high performance:

1. Knowledge and understanding
2. Skills and experience
3. Access to information, tools, and other resources
4. Motivation
5. Opportunities

The lack of any of these factors can result in substandard performance. In this approach, we determine which factors are acting as barriers to high performance and attempt to remove or remedy them.

The fourth approach is model-based. A causal model of the major variables and their dependencies must be developed. First determine the major factors or causal variables. If desired, use statistical methods to test for the strength of correlation. In addition, classify the factors as causal or affected; classify the variables as independent or dependent. Next, characterize the relationships as direct or inverse. Third, map the flow of causation. Fourth, look for feedback loops. If all the linkages are direct relationships, or if there are an even number of inverse linkages, the loop is inherently unstable and will eventually spiral out of control. This is to be avoided by redesigning the process — we want a stable process with minimum variation. Finally, run a computer simulation using the causal flow model.

Another variation is to use the process model in place of the causal flow model. Here, process activities will replace causal variables. By running a computer simulation, process model that can fairly accurately predict the results of proposed changes.

Step 3 — Generate Potential Solutions

Both divergent thinking and convergent thinking are necessary for effective problem-solving and creative thinking. Divergent thinking is the process of generating ideas. Convergent thinking is the process of eliminating the weak alternatives and focusing on only the most promising ones. This one-two punch — divergent followed by convergent thinking — is the essence of creative thinking. It should be applied in many settings, including problem-solving, decision-making, and learning.

The objective in this step is to generate as many ideas as possible, suspending judgment until step four, Evaluate and Select Solution. Researchers have found that the quantity of ideas generated is directly related to the ultimate quality of the solution. As idea generation dries up, ideas are combined and organized, and duplicates are weeded out.

Several techniques from creative thinking have proven valuable:

- Enhanced Brainstorming
- Analogies/Metaphors
- Interrogatories (5W/H — who, what, where, when, why, how)
- Problem Reversal
- Wishful Thinking

Most of the creative thinking techniques presented here are intended to be used by a four to ten person group. However, most techniques can be used directly or adapted for use by individuals.

Step 4 — Evaluate and Select Solution

Convergent thinking is the process of eliminating the weak alternatives and focusing on only the most promising ones. In this step we want to reduce the many ideas and alternative solutions generated in Step 3 down to just one or two good solutions. Decision analysis techniques, as well as creative thinking techniques, are particularly valuable for evaluating, and prioritizing, and selecting the best solution given the problem environment. Decision Analysis involves quantitative techniques that rely on Utility and Probability Theory. Creative thinking uses more qualitative methods, such as Pro/Con/Fix, Multi-Voting, Force-Field Analysis, and Causal Flow Analysis.

Regardless of which techniques are selected for this step, the evaluation criteria must first be determined. This may already be included in the technique, but using the following approach is recommended. Examine the criteria discussed in the criteria listed above in step 2, Analyze Problem, of this task.

Decision Analysis is usually reserved for complex problems where arriving at the best possible solution has great value. Once the evaluation criteria have been determined, users apply Utility Theory to determine the relative importance of each factor and assign weights accordingly. Users then exhaustively list all the possible outcomes/solutions, and estimate the fractional probability of each scenario actually occurring. According to Probability Theory, the probabilities attached to each outcome must sum to one. Next, the weights and probabilities are multiplied, and then totalled into Expected Values for each outcome. The outcome with the largest Expected Value is the best solution.

The Pro/Con/Fix technique organizes the problem elements so that each element can be analyzed and evaluated separately and systematically. First, each possible outcome/option/solution is listed as above. Then each option is evaluated as follows:

1. List all the Pros — positives, benefits, merits, and advantages
2. List all the Cons — negatives, risks, and disadvantages
3. Consolidate the Cons — merge similarities and eliminate redundancies
4. Neutralize the Cons — find measures or fixes to either convert Cons into Pros or neutralize Cons

Finally, compare the Pros and remaining Cons for all options, and select the Test and Implement Solution.

Step 5 — Test and Implement Solution

During this step we want to confirm that a good result was reached by building, testing, comparing, modifying, and improving our solution. In addition, the solution must integrate easily into the existing business system environment — that is, it can be implemented. For more details, see Chapter 11.

Step 6 — Document and Share Results

The results of your problem-solving efforts, whether successful or not, must be documented and then shared with others. Structure your documentation into problem, solution, and lessons learned categories, or organize around the six-step problem-solving approach used here. Document how you did the problem-solving — what tools and techniques you applied, what worked and what didn't, and hypothesize why. Document and retain your working papers from flipcharts, stickies, etc. — this work is often reusable later on.

It is crucial to promptly share and report problems, opportunities, solutions, and other results of problem-solving efforts to peer sites and to process and functional owners. This is a critical input to Chapter 10, Organizational Learning and Innovation.

Suggested Readings

Birchall, D. and Lyons, L. *Creating Tomorrow's Organization: Unlocking the Benefits of Future Work*. Pitman Publishing. 1995.

Couger, D. *Creativity and Innovation in Information System Organizations*. Course Technology. 1996.

Leonard-Barton, D. *Wellsprings of Knowledge: Building and Sustaining the Sources of Innovation*. Harvard Business School Press. 1995.

Mabey, C. and Iles, P., ed. *Managing Learning*. Routledge. 1994.

Marquardt, M. *Building the Learning Organization*. McGraw–Hill. 1996.

Marquardt, M. and Reynolds, A. *The Global Learning Organization: Gaining Competitive Advantage through Continuous Learning*. Irwin. 1994.

Martin, J. *Cybercorp: The New Business Revolution*. AMACOM. 1996.

Martin, J. *The Great Transition: Using the Seven Disciplines of Enterprise Engineering to Align People, Technology, and Strategy*. AMACOM. 1995.

VanGundy, A. *Idea Power: Techniques and Resources to Unleash the Creativity in Your Organization*. AMACOM. 1992.

References

1. Garvin, D. "Building a Learning Organization." *Harvard Business Review.* July-August 1993.
2. Nonaka, I. and Takeuchi, H. The Knowledge-Creating Company: How Japanese Companies Create the Dynamics of Innovation. Oxford University Press. 1995.
3. Marquardt, M. and Reynolds, A. *The Global Learning Organization: Gaining Competitive Advantage through Continuous Learning.* Irwin. 1994.
4. Couger, D. *Creativity and Innovation in Information System Organizations.* Course Technology. 1996.
5. Birchall, D. and Lyons, L. *Creating Tomorrow's Organization: Unlocking the Benefits of Future Work.* Pitman Publishing. 1995.
6. Jashapara, A. "Competitive Learning Organization: A Quest for the Holy Grail." *Henley Management College Working Paper.* England. 1993.
7. Marquardt, M. *Building the Learning Organization.* McGraw–Hill. 1996.
8. Kolb, D. *Experiential Learning.* Prentice-Hall. 1983.
9. Martin, J. *The Great Transition: Using the Seven Disciplines of Enterprise Engineering to Align People, Technology, and Strategy.* AMACOM. 1995.
10. Clemmer, J. *Pathways to Performance: A Guide to Transforming Yourself, Your Team, and Your Organization.* Prima Publishing. 1995.
11. Leonard-Barton, D. *Wellsprings of Knowledge: Building and Sustaining the Sources of Innovation.* Harvard Business School Press. 1995.
12. Hayes-Roth, F., et al. *Building Expert Systems.* Addison-Wesley. 1983.

10 Applying Innovative Information Technology

We must develop systems that combine the expressiveness and procedural versatility of symbolic systems with the fuzziness and adaptiveness of connectionist representations.

— Marvin Minsky

Introduction

This chapter is mostly for CIOs and their technical advisors, the IS department, and any closet techies. If you can safely delegate this work to your trusted IS department or contract it out, you can skip all but the innovative business applications section at the end. On the other hand, if you want to know what it will take and how to do it, then read on.

In Chapters 6 through 9 we have described how to locate and capture existing knowledge from available sources, how to conceptually organize and structure a living corporate memory, how to best share and use the corporate memory for training and performance, and finally, how to create new knowledge from experimentation, discovery, creative thinking, and lessons learned.

It is our belief that most tacit knowledge and expertise contained in the minds of domain experts and in the policies, processes, structures, and culture of the organization, can be explicitly represented in software and be made available to all employees. In this chapter we will show how much of these human and manual artifacts can be recreated and enhanced on-line using innovative IT. In addition, we will discuss how new knowledge and relationships can be discovered by computers.We also believe that most of the value creation that is possible from applying IT comes from AI disciplines. This belief is founded on several observations:

- Most IS departments and their business counterparts do not understand the huge opportunities that they are ignoring.
- Most IS departments and their business counterparts do not develop good business requirements, nor do they have a method for so doing.
- Nearly all organizations do not have a clue how to extract and represent knowledge from domain experts.
- Most IS departments have only one or two ways to represent knowledge, and no vehicle for representing expertise.
- Most organizations do not incorporate innovative IT (mostly AI) in the reengineering of their business systems. This especially applies to decision-making, scheduling, and problem-solving — all tasks at which Expert Systems excel.

IT Assessment

The IT assessment measures the availability and capability of computing and communication resources. This assessment also determines the relative maturity of the IS organization. There are many dimensions involved in an IT assessment:

- Business requirements determination
- Architecture and standards
- Hardware: Computer and peripherals
- Systems software and interface
- Communications
- Databases and textbases
- Procedural-based software applications
- AI-based, intelligent software applications
- Help desk

First, who determines the business requirements for a project? Second, is there an information system architecture and related standards? Is the architecture open or closed? Is there compliance with the standards and do they add net-value to the IS services delivered to customers? Third, what percentage of employees are engaged in knowledge work or frequently need information, and therefore need a computer? And what percentage of knowledge workers have a computer and related peripherals? Does the IT platform meet the customer's needs? Fourth, do the systems and office automation software, office software, and interface add value and are they easy to use? Fifth, what is the status of communications? Is there a corporate-wide communications network? What percentage of employees with computers get e-mail? What percentage have Internet access, IS groupware, or other collaborative software in use?

Sixth, what information resources are available on-line? What is their frequency of use? Do users believe existing databases and textbases provide good value to meet organizational needs? What information do users need, but is not available? How easy is it to access and retrieve information? What types of data models are used: flat, relational, network, hierarchical, or object? Is information engineering used to develop databases? Are textbases flat or use hypertext and multi-media? Seventh, are routine tasks automated, and do tools exist to help workers? Are there transaction processing systems that were designed using structured design or information engineering methods? Are there procedurally-coded process control, scheduling, and decision-support systems? Eighth, what software applications are developed using Knowledge Engineering techniques such as Knowledge Elicitation and Knowledge Representation schema? What percentage of applications are based on expert systems and AI disciplines? How often are the following AI techniques used: Object Technology/Model-Based Reasoning, Rule-based Systems, Case-based Reasoning, Uncertainty, Utility, Natural Language, Text Generation, Intelligent Tutoring Systems, Machine Learning, and Knowledge Discovery and Data Mining? Do Knowledge Repositories and IPSS exist? Last, is there a help desk to assist users? How satisfied are the users? Does the help desk cover just the IT infrastructure, or does it also help users to operate the applications software and to navigate through the system?

The IT Prerequisite: The IT Infrastructure

Having an installed IT platform accessible by all employees is an important prerequisite. Without an IT infrastructure, it will prove impossible to fully leverage and share the knowledge and expertise in the organization. This infrastructure is best realized through a Network or Client/Server Architecture, preferably structured and organized with Object Technology. All employees have workstations capable of seamlessly reaching all services needed to support their work. This would probably require daily downloading of data and applications from a variety of local and remote servers through the organization's Intranet, an internal Internet. These servers would contain suites of office automation software; custom software applications; databases; text bases; case, rule, and model bases; and image repositories. Later on, more extensive Knowledge Repositories are created, and finally IPSS.

Guidelines for Identifying Promising Expert Systems

If you will recall, we discussed the nature of expertise and its characteristics in Chapter 5. In Chapter 7 we described the cognitive knowledge schema used to organize a corporate memory. In Chapter 9 we used Knowledge Elicitation techniques to extract tacit knowledge and expertise from the minds of domain experts. Now we will explain how to convert those cognitive schema into manipulatable symbolic formats using Knowledge Representation methods.

Now we will explain how to automate that expertise into online advice using Expert Systems (ES). Many of the abstract concepts from prior chapters rely on ES to realize their potential. ES are computer programs created to manipulate symbolic knowledge in narrow domains in order to solve specific problem and decision situations. Beckman[6] has developed a method for identifying and applying promising ES for business applications. In his classification system, there are three general types of ES (reiterating from Chapter 7:

1. Case-Based
2. Rule-Based
3. Model-Based

Case-Based Reasoning (CBR)

CBR is very tolerant of missing and conflicting data. Knowledge Discovery and Database Mining techniques can often generalize, induce, and transform cases, or portions of cases, into useful rules.

Case-Based Reasoning should be used when:

- The solution alternatives explicitly can be enumerated
- Numerous examples of worked cases exist that cover domain
- No domain model or theory exists
- Experts represent domain in terms of cases
- Human experts or expertise are not available
- Situational information is conflicting, uncertain, or missing
- Knowledge is volatile and dynamic
- Domain knowledge and expertise already captured by past cases
- Workforce experience and performance are low
- Need a fast way to acquire domain knowledge
- Want to illustrate an outcome or explanation with an example
- Want to contrast and compare potential solutions
- Want to assess pros and cons of a situation
- Want to test a theory or solution with cases

Rule-Based Systems (RBS)

RBS use many small slivers of knowledge organized into conditional if-then rules. Inference engines for RBS are either goal-driven, backward-chaining, or data-driven, forward-chaining, depending on the type of application or generic task. Rules often represent heuristics — shortcuts or rules-of-thumb for solving problems. Regarding the amount of structure, RBS fall in-between CBR and MBR — rules of thumb are abstracted and generalized from experience into small chunks of knowledge. Both CBR and RBS can be developed incrementally and can provide some value in an unfinished state. Sometimes RBS can be transformed into objects or frames using Knowledge Discovery and Database Mining techniques.

Rule-Based Systems should be used when:

- Human experts think in terms of rules and heuristics
- Task involves decision-making, problem-solving, heuristics, or judgment
- Domain is complex and substantial expertise exists
- Knowledge is stable and is well- or semi-structured
- Expertise is primarily symbolic, not numeric
- Human experts are willing and available for knowledge elicitation
- Work performance and product quality are poor

- Employee turnover is high and training is expensive
- Impending loss of domain experts

Model-Based Reasoning (MBR)

MBR provides a representational and conceptual framework for knowledge that defines both knowledge structures and inferencing methods. MBR defines and structures relevant domain objects/concepts, their attributes, and their behaviors in order to organize work in complex domains and perform simulations. MBR also defines the relationships between the objects in terms of class hierarchies, composition, and causation. The most basic knowledge structure, governing all types of knowledge, is the <Object Attribute Value> triple.

MBR encompasses, represents, and organizes all types of knowledge, including CBR and RBS, as well as databases, text, images, and other media. Types of MBR are Object-based, Frame-based, and Domain-specific; MBR models can also be categorized as Quantitative or Qualitative. MBR requires a well-structured, well-understood domain theory. In simulation, MBR components are often so tightly linked together that MBR has limited value without a completed model. MBR is also very useful for organizing and structuring complex domains and work processes.

Model-Based Reasoning should be used when:

- A consensus framework of concepts and domain theory exist
- Business processes, methods, and events need to be represented and modeled
- Want to represent and organize large-scale, complex systems
- Want to simulate performance and side-effects from future Work System design
- Want to control, monitor, and measure information workflows
- Want to represent, organize, and integrate elements of Knowledge Repositories and related Performance Support Systems
- System navigation and presentation are important
- Environment and data are relatively dynamic
- IT infrastructure uses a client/server architecture
- Results from knowledge elicitation and acquisition need to be organized

Knowledge Repositories

A Knowledge Repository (Beckman, 1996) is an on-line, computer-based storehouse of expertise, knowledge, experience, and documentation about a particular domain of expertise. In creating a Knowledge Repository, knowledge is collected, summarized, and integrated across information sources. Knowledge Repositories contain many types of knowledge that can be represented by a number of standard formats. As we discussed in Chapter 7, the AI discipline of Knowledge Representation consists of knowledge structures and reasoning mechanisms that can structure, organize, summarize, and integrate virtually any type of experience, expertise, knowledge, information, or data about a particular specialty or domain.

Types of Domain Knowledge

A Knowledge Repository consists of many different types of knowledge, experience, expertise, and information:

- Directory of knowledge sources and skill sets
- Plans and schedules
- Procedures
- Principles, guidelines
- Standards, policies
- Causal models (MBR)
- Process maps and workflows (MBR)
- Information/data stores
- Decision rules (RBS)
- Performance measures and other data
- Worked cases (CBR)
- Designs of business system components
- Stakeholder and customer profiles: needs, values, expectations, perceptions
- Products and services: features, functionality, pricing, sales, repair
- Domain workforce profiles: knowledge, experience, preferences, interests, performance
- Domain best practices
- Current state assessments
- Competitive intelligence

- Environmental monitoring/scanning
- Lessons learned

Input and Output Modes

Knowledge can be entered and accessed through a variety of possible Input and Output Modes:

- User Interface
- External databases
- Print media
- Images and video
- Audio
- Sensors/Signals
- Multi-media
- E-mail
- Voice-mail
- Fax-mail
- EFT/EDI
- TDI — Technical Data Interchange

Knowledge Structures in the Repository

The major knowledge structures that can exist in a Knowledge Repository are:

- Models
- Rules
- Cases
- Databases
- Text
- Images

A Knowledge Repository can consist of a number of different Knowledge Representations — knowledge structures, as well as reasoning mechanisms to make inferences and draw conclusions from the existing knowledge:

- Domain Dictionary: Objects and Their Meanings; Concept Hierarchy
- Image-Base: Digitized Images and Video
- Text-Base: Books, periodicals, manuals, handbooks, news feeds
- Document-Base: Hypertext, Form Templates

- Data-Base: Relational, Network, Hierarchical, Flat
- Case-Base: Worked prototypical examples for decision-making and problem-solving
- Rule-Base: Heuristics, Decision-making, Problem-solving, Definitional Knowledge
- Script-Base: Events, Stereotypical Behavior, Procedures
- Object-Base: Concepts, Entities, Objects; Attributes and Values; Behaviors; Relationships; Inheritance
- Workflow Base: Process Maps
- Model-Base: Causal Models, Framework for Business System

A Black-Board Architecture serves as a sophisticated query language and is used to decide which knowledge sources should be invoked, and how to control, coordinate, and summarize their outputs. This means that redundant information can be eliminated, results can be explained, and conflicting results can be presented as alternatives.

Integrated Performance Support Systems (IPSS)

We have been discussing the application of ES at the micro-level in an organization. It is also possible to consider the totality of workforce needs by designing Integrated Performance Support Systems (IPSS) that make use of various AI disciplines. IPSS can be categorized into the following services (after Winslow and Bramer[3])

- Infrastructure: organizing and structuring the work environment (MBR and Knowledge Repositories)
- Controller: monitoring, coordinating, and controlling IPSS services (Black-Board Architecture)
- Navigation: human-computer interaction (MBR)
- Presentation: users can tailor and customize data and other service aspects (MBR)
- Acquisition: capturing knowledge, cases, opinions, learnings, and sensory data in various media forms and transforming them to an internal form (smart templates)
- Advisory: provides advice, reminders, assistance (RBS and CBR)
- Instruction: help, job aids, tutoring, training (MBR, RBS, and CBR)
- Evaluation: assessing and certifying based on performance measures, automated QA, and administered tests (CBR and RBS)

- Reference: directories of workforce and organizational domain knowledge and expertise, interests and preferences, and performance, as well as source of intranet, Internet, and other databases and information
- Search: Keyword, semantics, CBR, and other AI search engines

In addition to ES, other AI disciplines involved in providing IPSS include Intelligent Tutoring, Knowledge Discovery and Learning, Intelligent Information Retrieval, Smart Form Templates, Uncertainty, as well as Speech Recognition, Intelligent OCR, Natural Language Understanding through Conceptual Dependencies, and Text Generation.

One interesting issue is when should the IPSS actively intervene in the employee's performance of work.

Knowledge Transformations

Recent work by Beckman[1] has shown that it is often possible to automatically transform knowledge from one form to another. The idea involves upgrading knowledge from a lower state, such as cases, to a higher form, such as rules, by using knowledge discovery techniques from Machine Learning, Uncertainty, Probability, and Statistics.

Recent research by Zarri[2] indicates how unstructured text in the form of documents can be translated into more useful forms using the AI discipline of Natural Language Understanding. The translation into conceptual forms of Semantic Nets, Frames, and Conceptual Graphs results in a sophisticated indexing scheme. Once in this "metadocument" form, queries can be formed to search and retrieve relevant textual information.

From a business standpoint, the key questions are how much value does knowledge in a certain form provide to an organization, and how much does it cost to acquire and/or transform that knowledge? Recall the Knowledge Hierarchy introduced in Chapter 6:

Inputs → Data → Information → Knowledge → Expertise → Capability

Each generic form of knowledge can be transformed into the next higher form:

Inputs → Data: At the lowest level, raw inputs of differing forms are digitized and then transformed into symbols or data. Raw inputs from humans, recorders, and sensor inputs are digitized for input into the

Knowledge Repository. The data level can be bypassed by using smart form templates to capture user inputs of concepts, facts, and text and then immediately validate them, directly transforming inputs into information. In a less frequent manner, knowledge and expertise can be entered directly into the Knowledge Repository by domain experts, bypassing both data and information levels.

Speech is converted into text via Speech Recognition and Natural Language Understanding grammar AI software. Images in the form of handwriting, printed text, pictures, and video are first digitized using scanners. Then Image Recognition software is used to interpret images and convert them into symbols and to identify specific humans with the images. Cursive, script handwriting as well as printed hardcopy can be converted into ASCII text via intelligent Optical Character Recognition (OCR) software. Image Recognition software is used in the security industry to positively identify approved employees or residents through facial features, iris features, voiceprints, or fingerprints. In another example, specialized codes, such as bar-codes, are read by special scanners and converted into symbols. Further, robots use Computer Vision to identify parts to pick from bins. In a final example, analog temperature readings are converted into digital numbers.

Data → Information: There are three types of data: text, facts, and codes. Data are transformed into information objects by giving them context and meaning through semantics and relationships. Data are also filtered, sorted, summarized, and formatted for relevance and fitness for use. Text is given meaning and transformed into symbolic concepts and relationships via Natural Language Understanding AI software. Facts are transformed into information by classifying and organizing them into larger structures such as conceptual and compositional. This tracks the representational change from facts <attribute value> to objects <object attribute value>. Code systems are interpreted via specialized software. The most common forms of information are databases for facts and codes, and conceptual graphs for text. Correspondingly, the interface style moves from command-based to icon-based.

Information → Knowledge: During this transformation, the emphasis is on capturing the reasoning methods, rather than on the knowledge structure. In addition to methods for reasoning about information, the knowledge category involves capturing process and procedural knowledge that is sequence dependent. Information can also be generalized and abstracted into theories and basic principles. During this transformation, causal and associational relationships are determined between the objects. The breadth of consideration is expanded from a collection of objects to an entire application knowledge domain. For example, worked cases can be transformed and generalized into rules by the application of induction machine learning. In another approach, a collection of cases is transformed into knowledge by the application of a similarity inference engine. Another example, rules are transformed into a causal or decision model.

Knowledge → Expertise: Knowledge is transformed into expertise by selecting knowledge that will provide accurate and fast advice. Transforming knowledge into expertise requires the optimization of performance under resource constraints. High performance requires the application of the most relevant and important knowledge to the problem situation. Constraints include time, cost, knowledge, and human resources. Expertise also involves learning and adaptability — the knowledge must evolve and improve over time — through experience and collaboration. Further, expertise requires the generation of text to explain, justify, and summarize the results and reasoning processes. Finally, expertise includes the ability to teach others.

Expertise → Capability: The final transformation requires the creation of Knowledge Repositories and Integrated Performance Support Systems from the integration of multiple knowledge sources. The scope of the expertise is expanded from a single domain to encompass all the relevant domains needed to provide an organizational capability such as new product development, customer service, or product production. The role also expands from a single domain expert to groups of cross-domain teams who collaborate, discuss, and argue about how best to perform core business processes. As we shall see in Chapter 11, organizations should be restructured as Centers of Expertise to supply practitioners to Project and Process Offices. For success, organizations need to learn through creativity, experimentation, and innovation.

Machine Learning

Machine Learning is a key AI discipline that creates new knowledge, expertise, and value. Machine Learning consists of software that can improve its performance, discover new concepts, and adapt their responses to new situations.

Learning can be done in batches (fixed) or incremental (dynamic). In our context, machine learning involves transforming knowledge to a higher, more valuable, level. The most common type of machine learning is induction. Induction takes worked cases and develops rules that will produce the best overall results on the training cases.

Jaime Carbonell[10] has identified four major paradigms or approaches to ML:

1. Inductive: Acquire concepts; generalize; uses positive and negative examples
2. Analytic: Deductive; case-based or analogical; Explanation-Based Learning (learning from a single example); multi-level chunking; iterative macro-operators
3. Genetic: Classifier; biological reproduction; natural selection
4. Connectionist: Neural networks

Recall the discussion of how mature and how structured a given knowledge domain is from Chapter 6. Carbonell explains that connectionist approaches work best in unstructured domains with many training examples, such as image or speech recognition. At the other extreme, analytical methods are best for noise-free, well-structured, knowledge-rich domains. In the middle, inductive and genetic techniques work best when domains are semi-structured with lots of examples. Image and speech recognition transforms bit maps and signals into symbols and words. For instance, intelligent Optical Character Recognition can take cursive, script handwriting and convert it into digitized characters.

Knowledge Discovery and Data Mining

One of the most exciting and profitable recent concepts in creating new knowledge is the fusion of techniques from the fields of statistics, exploratory data analysis, on-line analytical processing (OLAP), causal modeling, and machine learning. According to Fayyad, Piatetsky-Shapiro, and Smyth,[4] Knowledge Discovery in Databases (KDD) is the process of identifying valid, novel, potentially useful, and ultimately understandable patterns in data. KDD is a multi-step process involving data selection, preprocessing, transformation, mining, and interpretation/evaluation. The KDD process is interactive and iterative with many decisions being made by the user.

Data Mining is at the heart of the KDD process. Data mining is the fitting of models to, or determining patterns from, observed data.[4] The primary goals of data mining are better description and prediction of a domain from its available data. There are a number of data mining tasks:

- Classification
- Regression
- Clustering
- Summarization
- Dependency Modeling
- Change and Deviation Detection

There are also a number of data mining methods:

- Decision Trees and Rules
- Nonlinear Regression and Classification Methods
- Example-based Methods
- Probabilistic Graphical Dependency Models
- Relational Learning Methods and Use of Intelligent Agents

Implementing Innovative IT To Support KM

By applying innovative IT to support KM, we believe that leading-edge organizations can achieve market leadership, customer intimacy, superior operational performance, as well as higher profit margins. Beckman[6] has outlined how the IS department can evolve to support the KM program through four sequential, but overlapping stages:

Stage 1 — Establish an installed networked IT infrastructure for all employees

Stage 2 — Create enterprise-wide data, object, and knowledge repositories

Stage 3 — Automate and enable operations, management, and support activities

Stage 4 — Develop Integrated Performance Support Systems and Knowledge Discovery and Data Mining Applications

Stage 1 — IS and IT Infrastructure

It is not enough to identify and develop isolated ES applications for business applictions — all employees must be able to access them. The prerequisite is that there must be a networked IT platform installed across the organization to support the ES applications. Every employee is equipped with a workstation that supports complex computational, informational, and communication needs. Every employee can communicate electronically with all other employees, both as individuals and collaboratively in groups.

Powerful system navigation and information exploration tools such as those developed by Shneiderman[5] are available that use flexible keyword search, hypermedia, dynamic visual querying, and tree maps. Every employee is provided with a suite of standard office automation software including text processing, presentation graphics, spreadsheets, relational DBMS, calendaring, meeting schedulers, Web browsers, E-mail, voice-mail, and fax-mail. This standard software should be integrated with the custom IS.

Stage 2 — Knowledge Repositories

In stage 2, enterprise-wide relational and object models are created, populated, and regulated. Consistent corporate-wide data or object dictionaries are created. Existing on-line data are transformed and reformatted onto relational databases, or wrapped for object models. Because most data were previously kept on paper, a massive data entry effort may be required to populate the databases. Smart data-entry templates are available to ensure quality by checking for entity, validity, consistency, and reality.

Later, multi-media object repositories that hold data, text, graphics, images, full-motion video, audio, objects, cases, and rules have supplanted relational data models. Knowledge Repositories are built for special-purpose, functional, corporate, and external uses. ES and other AI software exist to translate from most media into text and to understand what the text means using intelligent OCR for document images, voice recognition for audio, vision understanding into textual features, and from text into meaning using natural language understanding.

Stage 3 — Automated and Support ES Applications

Stage 3 is completed through use of ES applications in the sections described below. Coupled with electronic audit trails, many routine decisions and tasks are automated within the organization, and many others are supported by ES. In marketing and sales, ES helps the organization to establish better relationships and partnerships with their customers, better match products to customer needs, and to increase profit margins through improved pricing. Outside the organization, customers have direct access to powerful ES tools provided by the organization to help them understand and purchase products as well as maintain and repair products. Many products also have embedded ES for improved performance and service.

Stage 4 — IPSS and Knowledge Discovery

In Stage 4, Centers of Expertise (COE) are formed that are responsible for the collecting, learning, organizing, and distributing of knowledge for core competencies and other domain specialities of importance to the organization. COE educate and certify workers in their specialties, provide qualified workers and consulting services both on-line and in person to clients, and set and enforce standards for their specialties. COE also create, maintain, and enhance Knowledge Repositories and IPSS through internal and external research, as well as employee and organizational feedback.

Other Artificial Intelligence disciplines are also applied to solve business problems. In particular, Machine Learning techniques are applied for dynamic optimization of resource allocation and workload scheduling applications, resulting in dramatic gains in performance. Machine Learning is also used for Knowledge Discovery and Data Mining,[4] as well as to detect trends in data, such as MIS data. Intelligent Assistants, combined with Natural Language Understanding and Text Generation, are used to search for, select, and summarize news stories on certain topics.

The most dramatic performance gains will come from the deployment of Integrated Performance Support Systems that provide employees with coordinated services for task information, advice, training, job aids, reference, and administrative and personal resources to meet organizational and individual needs. These services might include sophisticated automation of and/or support for task processing and structuring; tutoring; problem-solving; decision-making; and information analysis through Knowledge Discovery and Data Mining techniques.

Business Applications of Expert Systems

In this section, numerous examples of prototypical business applications of expert systems will be described. In no sense is this list exhaustive, and it is hoped that these applications may spur additional ideas from the reader. The section is organized around the Business System components.

Product Applications of Expert Systems

Many types of products can have expert systems embedded in them. For example, ES can be used to monitor the performance or health of engines, appliances, and computer systems, reporting problems to the owner or the manufacturer. In addition to monitoring, ES can make diagnoses and suggest repairs. In another type of application, ES are used to control and optimize the performance of many products. For example, ES controllers are used to minimize energy usage in air conditioners and clothes dryers. In control tasks, ES using Fuzzy Logic are most often employed.

Software products offer many opportunities to employ ES. E-mail and voice-mail can be screened using evaluating and filtering generic tasks so that the most important and urgent messages are presented first. In addition, the system might signal the user as to the sender and message topic on important messages. Many messages approximating junk mail can be automatically deleted. Some message categories, such as confirmation, may receive automated replies.

Intelligent meeting schedulers could be especially valuable. An electronic scheduler could determine likely participants from the topic and prior meetings. It would poll the electronic calendars of potential participants looking for the optimal time and place, taking into account prior commitments, interests, roles, and work relationships. The scheduler could also do some limited negotiation and rescheduling of subordinate calendars.

Customer Service Applications of Expert Systems

The customer service process is highly informational and thus affords numerous opportunities for applying ES. This process involves three stages: pre-sale, transaction, and post-sale. In the pre-sale stage, the customer collects product information, compares products, selects features, and makes the purchase decision. During the transaction stage, customers input their orders, and select payment, warranty, delivery, and installation options. During the post-sale stage, customers receive product training and advice, use the product, and request repairs. A toll-free or Internet customer service help desk can be used to integrate these various applications, as well as provide more personalized service by accessing customer profiles.

Product Comparison and Selection: During the pre-sale stage, a CBR application could assist customers in selecting the product and features that would best meet their needs. The CBR application would find the best match between customer needs, requirements, and constraints such as cost and time; and available options in the company's product line, including product and service features and options.

Electronic Salesman: Given an extensive Customer Knowledge Repository, a RBS could send out customized advertisements targeted to known customer needs and values. These marketing proposals could recommend follow-on and augmented products and services based on prior purchase history. Another option would be to use the Electronic Salesman as an assistant during telemarketing. For example, Sang Kee Lee[8] suggests a salesman expert system for the customized purchasing support of men's wear using an integrated approach of RBS and Constraint Satisfaction methods.

Delivery and Repair Routing Schedulers: In many retail and service industries, deliveries and repairs must be made at the customer's site. Knowledge of best traffic routes and times during rush-hour and off-peak traffic hours is essential. For deliveries, average installation times should be well-known; and for repairs, rough estimates can be made based on the diagnosis from the symptoms. Incidentally, the diagnosis also includes the parts that will likely be needed, so that return repair trips can be minimized. RBS, CBR, or specialized GIS MBR can be used to not only optimize the routing, but also to give customers much more precise time windows for meeting the service personnel.

Product Diagnosis and Repair: RBS and CBR applications exist in many domains that perform the generic ES tasks of diagnosis and repair. Automobile, mainframe computer, and elevator repair ES are typical examples. CBR can be especially useful because new worked cases can be added by the users.

Product Advice and Assistance: Customers very often need help with installing, assembling, configuring, using, and trouble-shooting complex products. Advice could be accessed through toll-free phone numbers in which customer service representatives serve as intermediaries between the ES and the customer. Examples of this approach are IRS's Taxpayer Service Assistant[7] and the American Express Credit Analyzer Assistant. The Internet and kiosks at retail outlets could be used to deliver advice directly — ranging from interactive tutorials to more specific job aids. For extensive tutorials, MBR and RBS are both usually needed. For more focused advice and assistance, either CBR or RBS can be used.

Process Applications of Expert Systems

All internal aspects of a reengineered enterprise are organized around the process component. Decomposition of the process structures and organizes the supporting Business System components. MBR, and in particular, Object Technology, can be used to represent the process workflows, as well as simulating the performance of future designs and experimenting with various design alternatives. As the causal relationships between the business system components are better understood, better models can be built to forecast and plan future organizational performance.

Once work is assigned to an individual employee or work group, work can be structured and controlled using integrated MBR workflow management software that guides employees through the required or suggested best practice procedure. If completion dates are in jeopardy, then a reminder will be sent to the employee and his/her manager so that work can be reassigned or rescheduled if necessary. The MIS module will capture data on all work in progress and all completed work.

Management Applications of Expert Systems

Many aspects of management can be automated, resulting in a higher level of performance than is possible from any human manager or management team. The management tasks with the largest potential gains include dynamic workflow modeling and simulation for process improvement; automated workload management for allocating, scheduling, and assigning cases; automated case management for work requiring multiple specialists; automated quality assurance; and analyzing and forecasting trends in measurement data.

Dynamic Workflow Modeling and Simulation: All business concepts, practices, and processes can be documented and available on-line as text, process maps, supporting work system elements, and process simulation models. In addition, all relevant measurement data, as well as performance standards and employee compensation criteria, will also be available on-line, and will be integrated with the process models. The Management Information System (MIS) will be integrated with the related process models. Thus, all employees will be able to access, design, and test new process models through simulation by modifying the input variables. Modeling and simulation software will assist in improving the work processes.

Automated Workload Management   Work that is informational in nature can usually be performed independent of location simply by transferring caseloads electronically between sites. To accomplish this, an enterprise-wide Object-Oriented MBR is used to structure, organize, and sequence the work. Then specialized algorithms can be selected by RBS and applied to level workloads dynamically enterprise-wide. When corporate workload leveling is combined with sophisticated workload allocation, scheduling, and assignment algorithms, large gains in productivity and staff utilization are possible.

Automated Case Management   Cases can be structured using MBR to represent several important variables in allocating and scheduling work: the amount, type, location-dependence, and timing of receipt of the work; the quantity, skills, prior performance, and availability of staff; and the required completion date and accuracy. CBR and/or RBS can be used to optimize work assignments as well as workforce development. When workloads are high and inventories are backing up, the scheduler module will assign new work to the highest performing specialists available at the lowest appropriate skill and experience levels. When workloads are low, the module will assign or suggest to managers that they assign developmental tasks to employees that stretch their abilities. The module can also be used to plan future workloads and resource needs.

Complex work requests may require processing from a variety of specialists, sometimes in a certain sequence. This system serves as the case manager, creating a virtual single point of contact for the client. For example, hiring an employee might include tasks such as ordering furniture and computers, getting security clearances and ID badges, performing orientation and initiation, and establishing payroll and benefits.

This system also allows customers to request a completion date that can be negotiated by a RBS module based on user priorities if the requested date cannot be met. The system can reschedule other work assignments and renegotiate related completion dates to meet a truly urgent request. The system also sends notifications to customers when it forecasts that agreed-to completion dates will not be met.

Automated Quality Assurance (QA): All work performed electronically can be automatically sampled and compared for quality. CBR software allows for the comparison of stereotypical cases against newly worked cases. Sampled cases that are very similar to stereotypical cases are assumed to be correct. Cases that are dissimilar are referred to managers and/or appropriate QA employees. New cases are reviewed for accuracy and method of solution. There are three possibilities: the new case is either incorrectly worked, represents a new type of work, or has a different valid or better solution method than exists in the case-base.

In addition to on-line QA, the evaluation module also can generate simulated test cases in certain situations. In real time, the evaluation module generates test cases or selects them from a case-base in response to recent errors in certain types of cases, or when analysis of performance measures indicates a problem. Test cases are sent to employees when QA or the manager detects errors. Test cases can also be sent to employees to evaluate recent training or the need for remedial training.

Analysis and Forecasting of Trends in Measurement Data: Standardized Management Information System (MIS) reports will provide raw and percentage change comparisons to the immediate prior period as well as the same period for the prior year for all requested levels. Exception reporting with user-set default settings or highlighted variances of specified sizes can be selected. Users will be able to customize the reports to suit their own preferences by changing a few parameters. Sophisticated user interface design will allow users to more easily browse, explore, or produce desired ad hoc requests.

A variety of techniques are available for analyzing the MIS results. RBS can detect significant variances in historical measurement data, and MBR can forecast future trends and problems based on causal or empirical relationships between measures. Text generation AI software can explain the variances in English prose. Process simulation MBR models can be used to predict the downstream consequences of the variances. Time-series Trend Analysis software also will be used to forecast future performance. Information access and presentation will have functionality similar to that described for external environmental scanning.

Workforce Applications of Expert Systems

There are many workforce applications that are better performed by computer or that provide intelligent support to the workforce. Many routine operational tasks of an informational nature can be partially or totally automated. More important are the uses of ES to empower front-line employees to make decisions once reserved for management. To ensure accountability and security, electronic audit trails and ES monitoring are used. Using CBR and RBS, job announcements and assignments can be made automatically with management providing criteria for content and selection. Employees indicate interest in and availability for positions and assignments, and the system evaluates applicant performance and capabilities to find the best matches to the needed requirements and skills. Automated employee appraisals already exist in some companies using agreed to standards and measurement criteria, as well as customer and peer evaluations.

Automation of Routine Work Routine, simple, boring tasks will be automated to the extent possible. Examples will be data entry, form correctness and completeness checks, and simple approvals. Employees will no longer process and control paper, but rather will provide value-added advice and services that require knowledge and judgment. Electronic templates, supplanted by RBS, will be provided to capture data from paper forms, immediately applying entity, validity, consistency, and reality checks to the data entered. The information captured will be stored in knowledge repositories for later use.

Empowering Employees Front-line employees will have immediate access to needed information sources on-line. They also will have expanded decision-making authority and responsibility for results. RBS and CBR can push decision-making down to the working level in many instances. ES can automate some decisions, as well as support most other decisions while leaving the human in control. An electronic audit trail can be kept of all personnel actions, purchases, and consequential decisions.

Automated Job Announcements and Assignments A job announcements database will list the skills, assignment duration, and project leader for specific projects. Employees will be able to proactively apply for assignments individually on-line or can request receipt of all announcements of a certain type by location and duration. Employees can use CBR to select the best match between their skills, experience, interest, and availability, and the characteristics of available positions. Project offices can also assign project development work automatically through use of RBS and CBR by determining the skills needed for the job, evaluating the applications submitted, and searching the skills inventory, employee leave, and employee career development data stores for available employees with the needed skills and performance. This approach will eliminate favoritism and promote true merit selection.

Automated Employee Appraisal A multiple perspective approach to appraisal, such as Kaplan and Norton's[9] Balanced Scorecard, is recommended. An automated employee appraisal system using this approach can be used to align enterprise-wide strategies with the compensation system. Performance metrics will be cascaded down from the enterprise-wide level into clusters of relevant supporting measures for each individual employee. Performance measures and Quality Assurance samplings will provide most information on employee performance. Information on training and education received by employees will also be on-line. Structured appraisal templates will be issued automatically by the system to peers, project managers, and functional experts. Responses, including free text, will be received, scored, and analyzed. Text Generation AI software can convert numeric scores, text, and other inputs into a written appraisal that the manager can use or modify, according to need.

Automation of Administrative Tasks Many personnel and administrative tasks will be automated, eliminating the need for most administrative managers and personnel. CBR software can be used by employees to select the most appropriate health benefits plan. Employees enter their requirements and preferences and the CBR returns the plans with the closest match on the features. An RBS module can be added to assist in choosing the features, as well as compute the likely plan cost of a number of desired features.

Personal Assistants Personal Assistants (PAs) can assist employees in a variety of tasks. PAs using RBS and CBR can screen and prioritize E-mail and Voice-mail messages, including the deletion of duplicate messages. Voice-mail can be first transformed into text using Speech Recognition software. Particular topics and individuals can be selected for priority sorting. Users will be able to create PAs to perform complex procedural tasks, information retrieval tasks, or monitor-and-search tasks that humans are not good at. PAs can continually roam the intranet and/or Internet searching for and retrieving topics of interest.

Intelligent servers will schedule meetings automatically by cooperatively working with other servers to arrange and rearrange individual schedules according to user preferences and manager requests. When there are scheduling conflicts, the RBS mediates between participants depending on the reporting relationships, urgency, and existing assigned work. Intelligent meeting schedulers can also suggest potential participants and meeting roles, as well as compose meeting agendas, depending on the topic, type of meeting, and prior meeting action items.

Suggested Readings

Beckman, T. *Applying AI to Business Reengineering Tutorial*. 146 pages. Presented at the World Congress on Expert Systems III. Seoul, Korea. February, 1996.

Fayyad, U., Piatetsky-Shapiro, G., Smyth, P., Uthurusamy, R., eds. *Advances in Knowledge Discovery and Data Mining*. MIT Press. 1996.

Kolodner, J. *Case-Based Reasoning*. Morgan Kaufmann. 1993.

Michalski, R. And Tecuci, G. *Multistrategy Learning*. Tutorial at American Association of Artificial Intelligence Conference. 1993.

Parsaye, K. and Chignell, M. *Expert Systems for Experts*. John Wiley & Sons. 1988.

Shneiderman, B. *Designing the User Interface: Strategies for Effective Human-Computer Interface*, 2nd ed. Addison-Wesley. 1992.

Waterman, D. in Hayes-Roth, F., Waterman, D. and Lenat, D., ed. *Building Expert Systems*. Addison-Wesley. 1983.

Weiss, S. and Kulikowski, C. *Computer Systems that Learn: Classification and Prediction Methods from Statistics, Neural Nets, Machine Learning, and Expert Systems*. Morgan Kaufmann. 1991.

Winslow, C. and Bramer, W. Future Work: *Putting Knowledge to Work in the Knowledge Economy*. Free Press. 1994.

References

1. Beckman, T. *Applying AI to Business Reengineering Tutorial*. 146 pages. Presented at the World Congress on Expert Systems III. Seoul, Korea. February, 1996.

2. Zarri, G.P. *Building Up and Making Use of Corporate Knowledge Repositories*. KAW '96 — Corporate Modelling and Enterprise Modelling Track. 1996.

3. Winslow, C. and Bramer, W. *Future Work: Putting Knowledge to Work in the Knowledge Economy*. Free Press. 1994.

4. Fayyad, U., Piatetsky-Shapiro, G., Smyth, P., Uthurusamy, R., eds. *Advances in Knowledge Discovery and Data Mining*. MIT Press. 1996.

5. Shneiderman, B. *Designing the User Interface: Strategies for Effective Human-Computer Interface*, 2nd ed. Addison-Wesley. 1992.

6. Beckman, T. "Expert System Applications: Designing Innovative Business Systems through Reengineering." *Handbook of Applied Expert Systems*. Liebowitz, J., ed. CRC Press. 1998.

7. Beckman, T. "An Expert System in Taxation: The Taxpayer Service Assistant." *Managing and Developing Expert Systems*. J. Liebowitz, ed. Yourdan Press. 1990.

8. Lee, S.K. "Salesman Expert System for Customized Purchasing Support." In *Critical Technology: Proceedings of The Third World Congress on Expert Systems.* Cognizant Communication Corp. 1996.

9. Kaplan R. and Norton, D. "The Balanced Scorecard — Measures that Drive Performance." *Harvard Business Review.* Jannuary–Februbary 1992.

10. Carbonell, J., ed. *Machine Learning: Paradigms and Methods.* MIT Press. 1990.

11 Implementing the Knowledge Organization

To put your ideas into action is the most difficult thing in the world.

— Goethe

The organization's function is to put knowledge to work — on tools, products and processes, on the design of work, on knowledge itself.

— Peter Drucker

The New Society of Organizations

Harvard Business Review

1992

Introduction

Now that we have a good idea of what the Knowledge Organization looks like and how it works, we will now look at how to implement these concepts in the workplace. This is not as easy as you might think. As Bernard Jaworski[1] has noted, there are few, if any, direct bottom-line benefits from Knowledge Management; many of the benefits are indirect. While the long-term benefits may be critical to the future success of an enterprise, there are only developmental and capital costs associated with building a Knowledge Organization. The argument must be made that Knowledge Management is fast becoming a competitive necessity — how much money and market share will your company lose by not adopting the concepts of the Knowledge Organization?

This is not a costing exercise for your Finance department or your accountants; this is strategic management done by your senior management. We know what Finance will say, "Prove its worth in advance." We also know that this is virtually impossible. Pre-development benefit, cost, and risk estimates on new large-scale initiatives are typically off by more than 50%. The most realistic estimates will come from similar external best practices that have been in production for over one year. However, this exercise can be valuable if it is used to guide development of benefits and minimize risks, rather than be a funding constraint. There is no reality to the benefits forecast until the first prototype is tested by the client.

To succeed in creating a working Knowledge Organization requires serious attention to doing a number of activities well. First, organizational and environmental assessments need to be conducted to determine where the biggest bang for the buck is. Then, the four prerequisites must be addressed — leadership, culture, expertise, and IT. Next, we will examine a new motivational system to overcome dysfunctional cultures. After this, we will look at the new organizational structures and work roles that will be needed to support this venture. The final sections will deal with actually building, testing, and implementing the Knowledge Organization, beginning with the demonstration prototype, continuing with the staged rollout, and concluding with the transition to normal operations.

The best theory and the best practices are useless unless you can implement them. Most large organizations and even some small ones are traditional bureaucracies. Many of the behaviors and motivations of bureaucracies are antithetical to the knowledge organization. For example, bureaucracies value loyalty over truth to the point where they will often penalize employees who attempt to point out the reality of the marketplace or the needs of customers. Decisions are often made by managers based on their position, rather than by professionals based on their knowledge and expertise. Bureaucracies control knowledge and information as a form of power rather than sharing it across the organization. Employees get ahead by pleasing their supervisors rather than their customers. Managers typically advance through office politics, rather than merit. The system for measuring departments, if one exists, focuses on the financials, rather than on the customer or the performance and capabilities of the workforce. In a bureaucracy, employees are punished for taking risks; creative thinking is ridiculed and discouraged.

In order to succeed in implementing knowledge organizations or any other large-scale improvement strategy, such as business reengineering or process improvement, you must first break the back of the bureacracy. The following sections have a variety of advice for transforming your organization into a market leader. First, the measurement and reward systems must be radically changed to truly motivate employees as is discussed in the section

A Framework for Improvement Systems. Next, new organizational structures need to be created: Process Teams, Centers of Expertise and Knowledge Networks. Then, an IT infrastructure must be established on which to place the Knowledge Repositories, Integrated Performance Support Systems, and Knowledge Discovery engines. Simultaneously, the Knowledge Management process must be developed and implemented. Finally, business improvement strategies should be implemented.

Organizational and Environmental Assessment

To gain a rounded picture of the organization and the environment in which it resides, a series of assessments should be performed. These assessments are used to determine what is or should be important to the enterprise now and in the future, as well as to uncover the largest gaps in organizational performance and customer value. Once determined, this assessment will point to the best choices for the initial knowledge domains and related Centers of Expertise (COE). Thus, assessments should be performed for the following categories:

- Strategic/Leadership
- Environment
- Performance
- Cultural
- Expertise
- IT

Strategic Assessment

The Knowledge Organization should support and be aligned with the business strategy. If the strategy is non-existent or not followed, it should be revisited. The primary lynchpin between the business strategy and the Knowledge Organization is Prahalad and Hamel's[8] concept of core competencies. These competencies should flow out from the strategic intent and vision.

Identify those existing core competencies that are important to current success and those necessary for future competition. Assess whether these competencies now exist and their strength. Daniel Tobin,[6] in *Transformational Learning*, has developed a comprehensive sourcing plan to buy, rent, and develop the needed core competencies that was discussed in Chapter 6.

The strategic assessment should tell you what is most important and what is most broken. Focus the majority of your efforts on the largest performance or customer value gap. Then decompose your core competencies into process capabilities, and similarly decompose those process capabilities into knowledge domains. You should now know which knowledge domains are most critical to the organization's continued success.

Environmental Assessment

Environmental scanning and competitive intelligence (Kahaner, 1996) are two knowledge-intensive areas that require continuous monitoring. While not quite as important as understanding customer needs, values, expectations, and perceptions, your ability to quickly identify and respond to strategic threats and opportunities is still crucial to success. These knowledge domains could also make for relatively quick returns on your capital investment in Knowledge Management.

Implementation Prerequisites

There are four prerequisites that you need to consider as you begin to implement the Knowledge Organization:

1. Executive Leadership and Commitment
2. Healthy Culture
3. Expertise
4. IT Infrastructure

Without sustained leadership and sponsorship, the transformation of the organization through knowledge, experience, learning, and innovation is unlikely. Leaders first must be exposed to and understand the benefits, costs, and risks. Then they must become convinced of the need for and value of Knowledge Management. Finally, they need to become committed sponsors.

Culture can often be the death knell for large-scale change efforts like Knowledge Management, not to mention threatening the continued existence of the organization. A dysfunctional culture must be repaired before attempting to create the Knowledge Organization. Otherwise, the cultural forces of the status quo will resist, reject, and sabotage such efforts until they fail. Very often, the motivational and reward systems must be revamped. Once these cultural and behavioral changes are well underway, only then should the implementation begin. An added benefit is that other large-scale improvement initiatives, such as business reengineering, also have greatly increased chances for success.

The cornerstone belief of the Knowledge Organization is that expertise is the only sustainable competitive advantage. Without sufficient expertise in core competencies and related knowledge domains, the chances of long-term success are greatly reduced. Not only must the expertise exist, but the experts must be recognized and given the opportunity to lead the enterprise in the areas where they excel. Those workers with operational expertise must lead and possibly manage the production processes. Those professionals whose expertise lies in strategic improvement strategies such as process improvement, total quality management, and reengineering, should lead and manage the large-scale initiatives such as the Knowledge Management and Organization efforts. The IT assessment and prerequisite is covered in Chapter 10.

Leadership

The following leadership activities will help build commitment for the Knowledge Organizations.

- Understanding the Value of Knowledge Management
- Learning from Internal Mentors, Other CEOs, and Consultants
- Visiting Success Stories
- Making a Commitment
- Building Support and Consensus
- Communication and Marketing
- Leveraging Opportunities

The Chief Knowledge Officer (CKO)

Ideally, in the future, companies might not need a separate executive and organization for managing knowledge because it has been internalized into the fabric of the enterprise's daily work. However, until then, the discipline of KM needs its own leader and support. According to Tom Davenport,[10] the CKO must embody several roles:

- Advocate or evangelist for knowledge and learning
- Designer, implementer, and overseer of an organization's knowledge infrastructure
- Primary liaison between external providers of information and knowledge

- Lead the design and implementation of a company's knowledge architectures

He also suggests that this KM group could report to the CIO or to human resources, but is better off being its own executive directorate. We believe that the Chief Knowledge Officer should have expertise in the disciplines of business reengineering, innovative IT, change management, as well as knowledge management.

Davenport[11] also points out that most of the major management consulting companies — Andersen Consulting, Ernst and Young, Price Waterhouse, Booz-Allen and Hamilton, and McKinsey — already have a CKO or Director of Knowledge Resources or Director of Intellectual Assets. Expertise and knowledge are not only the product and service, but also the core competence and major source of competitive advantage for all consulting companies. In addition, most management consulting firms have developed industry-specific practices that can be seen as the first practical examples of domain-specific COEs, often with online Knowledge Repositories of best practices.

Expertise-Based Planning and Decision-Making

As you might guess, we believe that consequential decisions must be made through the application of expertise, knowledge, and experience. Therefore, the new decision-makers will be domain experts, mostly professionals, rather than bureaucratic managers or administrators. This is a stunning change from the manner in which strategic decisions typically are made today in most large organizations.

In most traditional organizations, the executives at the top of a command-and-control hierarchy make all important decisions and also set policy on who and how lesser decisions should be made. However, executives and managers in traditional bureaucracies rarely have the requisite understanding or expertise to make good decisions — it is that simple. To believe that expertise that took professionals years to attain can be passed up the "food chain" for informed discussion and decision-making by general managers is ridiculous. Unfortunately, expertise and technical knowledge are all too often diminished by middle-level managers who are driven by "the bottom line," and dismissed by executives who only see "the big picture."

One need only to look at strategic decisions made at IBM or GM during the 1980s to understand the hubris and arrogance that executives all too often exhibit. And reality in the form of competitive bad news is usually not allowed into the boardroom for rational discussion. However, the classic case of all decision blunders was the Challenger space shuttle that was launched over the strenuous objections of the Thiokol engineers, who risked their careers in standing up against their management. You can still hear the excuses made by NASA and Thiokol managements. Ultimately, NASA violated their own decision protocol which was, "When in doubt, don't launch."

Issues dealing with resource allocation and contention, as well as work assignment and scheduling can often best be solved by using a marketplace bidding system. At the strategic level, the viability and profitability of existing products and services, and the development of new more promising products and services, should be frequently revisited and reassessed using a marketplace bidding system for resource allocation. For example, products that are declining and marginally profitable should be sold off or retired in favor of other products that are more profitable or very promising future products that need development. In a more localized example, bidding for work assignments can be done on the basis of availability, expertise, interest, and organizational need. Beckman[15] has described how this was done on the team level in the IRS Quality Office.

Most consequential decisions will involve many domains of knowledge. All of these domains must be represented by a domain expert to present their perspective and to argue and discuss the merits of their positions. For example, the decision to proceed with developing a business reengineering project requires, at a minimum, strategists, marketing, customers, IT, HR, finance, the specific processes involved, and all relevant disciplines. For important decisions with high impact, the best available expert from each category should be present.

We believe that a decision protocol needs to be established for each type of problem or opportunity. First, it is essential to document the decision-making process as it unfolds. Much can be learned and applied to similar future decisions. Second, for each decision type, the various COEs that need to be involved must be identified and documented. Next, we recommend using the innovative problem-solving process that is described later in Chapter 9. Finally, a model for the detailed decision process needs to be developed. Consensus is an ideal and a luxury that rarely will be reached; reacting to threats and capitalizing on opportunities often require that a vote be taken quickly. We suggest that a simple majority vote is sufficient to make decisions for problems that are urgent and well-understood. When there is both urgency and less certainty, then perhaps a 2/3rds majority vote might be more appropriate. Votes can be weighted for each COE based on prior experience and success.

Sharing Knowledge

In order to maximize the sharing and communication of knowledge, there are several organizational dimensions, in addition to IT, that must be addressed:

- Structure
- Culture
- Reward System

In *The Smarter Organization*, McGill and Slocum[3] describe the evolution of organizational forms in four phases: knowing, understanding, thinking, and learning. The earliest stage, knowing, is characterized by high control, enforced conformity, predictable routine behaviors, risk avoidance, and pursuit of efficiency. The authors refer to this form as "learning disadvantaged."

These Knowing Organizations, also called command and control hierarchical organizational structures, are notoriously poor at sharing knowledge. There are filters that prevent bad news or non-conforming ideas from moving up the chain of command, and there are filters from the top that prevent the sharing of bad news or sensitive information with the "troops" who don't have a "need to know." We believe that not only is this dysfunctional, but also is disasterous to the trust, respect, and openness needed to share both bad and sensitive information.

All too often the command and control hierarchy is reinforced by a bureaucratic culture. This culture is secretive, competitive, and polarized into a caste structure consisting of management, technical professionals, and the rest of the workforce. This culture engenders distrust, but it understands that knowledge is a source of power and believes that information should be hoarded by the purveyors of power — management.

Bob Buckman[4] realized some time ago that the hoarding of knowledge to achieve power must be reversed. Buckman utilizes a carrot and stick approach, mixing visible incentives with invisible pressure. What he created was an organization-wide bias towards teamwork and knowledge sharing. Early on, Buckman recognized and rewarded the 150 best knowledge-sharers by treating them to a high-profile trip to a resort to hear Tom Peters speak, and by giving them business gifts. In the next section we will discuss other methods to increase knowledge sharing through the construction of a new motivational system.

A Better Motivational System:
Transforming Bureaucracies into Knowledge Organizations

Beckman[9] has proposed that an integrated motivational system can solve many of the design, implementation, and performance problems that have plagued the large-scale improvement efforts of most organizations. Curiously, there are almost no references in the improvement literature to an integrated system of goals, development, performance, measurement, appraisal, and reward. We are convinced that this framework can improve organizational performance and capabilities. In addition, such a system would motivate, develop, empower, and reward employees. Further, this compensation system would be fair and provide adequate opportunities for demonstration of performance and development of capabilities. Such a motivational systems consists of several activities:

Step 1 — Set Strategic Goals and Objectives
Step 2 — Develop Measures and Standards
Step 3 — Create Opportunities
Step 4 — Monitor and Assess Measures
Step 5 — Reward Results

In *Step 1*, Set Strategic Goals and Objectives, strategic goals are expressed in mission and vision statements, and in strategic plans. Goals must be translated into operationalized objectives. Each objective may consist of several dimensions: functionality, quality, time, and cost. Objectives should also be aligned with the organizational hierarchy. Each objective will also be decomposed at multiple levels: business unit, division, work group, individual. The alignment of objectives with the strategic goals is essential.

In *Step 2*, measures provide focus, quantify objectives, and set standards. Objectives are quantified by developing measures to adequately express each dimension. Detailed measures are weighted and combined into indices that summarize a dimension or higher level objective. Measures should express the capabilities and performance of all aspects of the organization. In addition to customer and performance measures, workforce development and work environment measures should be formulated. All important aspects of the organization can be represented through the components of a business system.

In addition, there are four basic types of processes that may require differing emphases in the measures:

1. Operational
2. Developmental
3. Managerial
4. Support

Next, for each measure, a reasonable standard of performance should be set. Finally, the individual measures must directly support and align with the next higher level of measures, those with the objectives, and the objectives with the ultimate strategic goals.

In *Step 3*, Create Opportunities, management, in partnership with the workforce, must find opportunities for development, empowerment, and performance that meet both organizational and personal interests and objectives. Management must provide opportunities for all employees to develop skills, experience, and knowledge that can improve their performance and increase their capabilities. Without developmental knowledge and experiences, performance will be disappointing. In addition to developmental opportunities, management must provide opportunities for employees to demonstrate, practice, perform, learn, and improve their performance and capabilities.

Step 4, Monitor and Assess Measures, provides for both internal and independent monitoring and assessment. Measures of performance should be monitored by external groups with interests in the outcomes, or groups that are at least impartial. For example, customers, peer groups, and senior management are likely candidates for monitoring.

Step 5, Reward Results, is the most important activity in the framework. It is essential to measure what you reward, and reward what you measure. Otherwise, no strong motivational effect will be created. If new measures are needed, or if existing measures need modification, create or fix them as soon as possible. Rewards should take many forms, including money, recognition, time off, empowerment, work selection, advancement, and development. And rewards should celebrate successes, as well as desired behaviors such as collaborating, experimenting, risk-taking, and learning. Reward early and often. One interesting aspect of this framework is that results and outcomes are the objectives being managed, not processes. There are several advantages to this approach. First, by emphasizing outcomes — that is, products, services, and financials — the organization focuses on meeting customer needs and business needs, not internal functional or political needs. Second, it gives managers of each organizational unit the flexibility to organize their processes and enabling business system components to best fit their local needs and personal management style, but holds them accountable for meeting the outcomes. Third, the workforce is primarily rewarded for results, not for internals.

What is the most important thing you can and must do to change the existing culture and mindsets so that they are receptive, supportive, and committed to the precepts of the knowledge organization? Motivate everyone by providing equal opportunities and development, as well as just appraisal and rewards. Management must measure and reward the performance, behaviors, and attitudes that are needed and desired. It is essential to measure what you reward, and reward what you measure.

So you might ask, well, what should get rewarded? We believe in applying Kaplan and Norton's Balanced Scorecard approach[2] to both measures and rewards. This approach is then combined with our core values of providing good value to the customer, serving the customer, high performance, leading with expertise, innovation, and sharing and cooperating. Therefore, we believe you should reward:

- Customer satisfaction
- High performance
- Personal knowledge and expertise
- Teamwork and sharing of expertise and knowledge
- Creating new and extending existing knowledge and expertise
- Using and applying the knowledge and expertise in the Knowledge Repository
- Proactive problem solving and problem prevention

What you should not reward (and could consider punishing):

- Buck passing
- Conformance and compliance behavior — passive resistance
- Internal competition

- Bureaucratic, controlling behaviors
- Power grabbing and turf battles

Measures provide focus, operationalize goals, and set standards. A multi-tiered, balanced scorecard approach to measurement seems most effective. Rewards should take many forms, including money, recognition, time off, empowerment, work selection, advancement, and development. And rewards should celebrate successes, as well as desired behaviors such as collaborating, experimenting, risk-taking, and learning. Reward early and often.

The Balanced Scorecard approach[2] has these basic measurement dimensions:

1. Customer
   — Value (Product, Service, Price)
   — Satisfaction
2. Financial
   — Expenses
   — Income
   — Net Earnings
   — Net Worth
3. Process
   — Quality
   — Time
   — Cost
   — Capacity
   — Flexibility/Adaptability
4. Workforce (added by many organizations)
   — Development
   — Empowerment
   — Motivation
   — Collaboration, Sharing, Teamwork
5. Learning
   — Core Capability
   — Expertise
   — Knowledge
   — Innovation

New Organizational Structures

Organizational development theorists have had a field day proposing new organizational structures to better serve new management and work configurations and differing corporate cultures. With names like Spider's Web, Inverted Pyramid, Shamrock, Noetic, Virtual, and Empty Shell, most of these new forms were devised to meet a specific need or function. What all these forms have in common is their disavowal of the hierarchical functional/departmental organizational structure, and they tend to share attributes of a Network form.

Another novel organizational form is the the *Practice* concept. In recent years, this organizational structure has been mos widely used by management consulting firms. This form was introduced at the National Security Agency (NSA) in 1995.[16] From the start, there has been overwhelming interest in Practice Centers from senior managers. This concept has proven to be the best way to share knowledge and expertise across Directorates within the Agency. Knowledge is shared through technical forums, symposiums, meetings, internal newsletters, and email. To date, there are 11 Centers with about 400 employees participating in them. The most successful Practice Centers combine participant energy with senior management support.

Because we believe that knowledge and expertise are the most important determinant of organizational success, our proposal for an effective organizational design centers around a new organizational type, the Center of Expertise (COE). A COE is similar to a practice center, but with "teeth."

In order to take full advantage of the Knowledge Management process, new organizational structures need to be created. Most important are the Centers of Expertise (COE) that are organized around each knowledge domain and attend to the care and feeding of the Knowledge Repositories. The Knowledge Organization requires greatly flattened hierarchies being reformed into a network of strategy, project, process, and COE groups.

Centers of Expertise (COE)

Beckman[13] has developed the concept of a Center of Expertise (COE) for each knowledge domain, discipline, or subject matter specialty. Each COE has several roles:

- Create, research, improve, and manage the domain Knowledge Repository
- Set and enforce standards, methods, and practices for each domain discipline
- Establish partnerships and align/coordinate interests with related COE specialties, projects, and processes, as well as negotiate conflicts between these entities
- Assess workforce competency and performance, identify gaps, and remedy deficiencies
- Support, develop, and enable the workforce by providing educational and consulting services, as well as coaching and tools
- Supply competent workers to staff projects and processes through assignment, hiring, outsourcing, and developing

You could say that the COE replaces the function in a matrixed management environment. Employees are developed and certified by COEs as competent in a domain to perform jobs to which they are assigned. Although most employees have only one primary COE to which they belong, they also receive training and support from those COEs that contribute to performing a given job type.

COEs are the sole source for staffing projects and processes within the organization. If insufficient qualified employees are available internally to staff an initiative, then they have the authority to either hire new staff or bring in temporary workers to make up the shortfall. Clearly, COEs must work closely with project and process offices, as well as business strategy, to ensure that adequate numbers of qualified staff will be available when needed. Each COE is funded through charge-backs from the office receiving the staff. The receiving offices are considered the customers of the COE and are a primary source for employee and COE performance feedback and evaluation. Whenever staff are not engaged in project or process work, then they are back at the COE enhancing their knowledge and expertise, as well as being debriefed to accumulate their learnings.

Initially, COEs can be staffed with one permanent domain expert and detailed-in experts from other peer working groups. COEs ultimately replace functions regarding their specialties of knowledge and expertise, while processes replace functions regarding their performance obligations. Finally, project and program offices replace the functions in their limited ability to develop new business systems.

Each COE is led by a team of true domain experts. If you do not have such employees, hire them or use contractors to aid in developing sufficient internal expertise. These directors are responsible for implementing and executing all six roles of the Centers of Expertise. All six roles must be covered, even if some directors lead two or three roles.

Knowledge Repository We have described in some detail how knowledge can be collected, extracted, and created, and then stored in domain Knowledge Repositories. Assign your combined best conceptual thinker, synthesizer, researcher, and high-performing domain expert to the care and feeding of the Knowledge Repository. This is the primary objective on which the other roles rely. This domain expert also should be articulate, able to elicit tacit knowledge from other practitioners, and be comfortable with IT and information systems.

Standards and Practices This director should be a high-performer and have broad experience in the domain. S/he should have a more practical mind-set than the Knowledge Repository director, and be current on industry standards and accepted practices. In addition, s/he should be able to negotiate and compromise when appropriate with other domains on setting standards. This director should be able to write clearly and develop guidelines and detailed procedures where needed for guiding novice and less experienced practitioners.

Relationships and Alignment A traditional manager with decent domain knowledge levels and excellent interpersonal skills should establish partnerships and supplier/customer relationships with other COEs. This director should facilitate linkages between Knowledge Repositories, as well as lead negotiations in settling disputes between COEs.

Assess Workforce The performance and capability of the existing workforce and of any contract employees must be periodically assessed. There also may be testing and certification of understanding, knowledge, and expertise. This director is expected to identify performance and expertise gaps in the workforce, and develop and implement the solutions, such as training, to remedy them. In addition, s/he leads the employee appraisal and compensation process using the Balanced Scorecard approach[2] described later.

Support and Develop Workforce   The leader of this role must be a true domain expert. Next to the Knowledge Repository, this role requires the most mastery of the domain. This director also must be skilled in educational methodologies, adult learning, and capable of developing and delivering courses and curricula. In addition, s/he should be adept at spotting opportunities to develop on-line consulting services and tools for the workforce.

Supply Staff   This role requires the abilities of a competent domain specialist, and a human resources manager with a specialty in recruiting. To adequately support the project and process offices with qualified staff, this director should be a master at forecasting and anticipating resource needs. In addition, s/he should have excellent recruiting abilities and a sense of where talented contract professionals can be found.

Organizational Structure by Work Type

Beckman[9] has posited that there are five basic types of work performed by every organization:

1. Strategy
2. Development
3. Production
4. Customer Support
5. Support

Each knowledge domain is represented by a separate COE, and each work type requires many different COEs to supply needed human and machine knowledge and expertise. The COE is a foundational type of unit — each one can support part of the five differentiated work types and organizational structures above it.

Production Processes

Production processes for the enterprise should be structured around products — not functions, not processes, and not customers. Handoffs, ownership, and turf battles kill high performance in the traditional functional bureaucratic structure. Organizing around core business processes works better if there is real ownership, but there often tends to be a lack of focus on products and customers. James Martin[5] in his book, *The Great Transition,* has suggested that most types of work can be best organized around customers as value streams. We differ with his concept for two reasons: (1) Good customer service can be better organized and delivered as a centralized entity outfitted with customer personalized points-of-contact, and (2) Multiple product lines that might be needed by a customer makes this approach duplicative, unwieldy, and inefficient. However, the suggested organization by product works best only after extensive market research by the Business Strategy and Customer Service work roles to determine customer needs, core competencies, and product lines.

Customer Support Process

According to Earl Naumann,[12] there are three basic stages involved in the customer support process:

1. Research
2. Purchase
3. Service

During the research or presale stage, the customer gathers information and advice in order to make a purchase decision. Dalrymple and Parsons[14] further subdivide this predecisional stage into three parts:

1. Recognition of problem or need
2. Search for alternatives and information
3. Buyer's mental evaluation of alternatives

In many industries, marketing through samples, test use, and adoption by demanding customers can be very effective in influencing the purchase decision. The organization's ability to customize and personalize the product or service can also influence this decision.

During the purchase or transaction stage, there are several aspects to consider:

- Pricing and payment options
- Financing and credit authorization
- Guarantees and return policy
- Scheduling delivery and installation
- Ease of transaction

Finally, during the service or post-sale stage, the following activities are critical:

- Delivery and installation
- Training, consulting, and help desk support
- Repairs and upgrades
- Customer satisfaction: complaints, feedback, and suggestions

Support Functions

Support functions serve internal customers. Support functions consist largely of infrastructures that permeate, affect, and hopefully enable every facet of the enterprise. Virtually every organization needs these functions:

- Management
- Human Resources
- Finance
- Information Technology
- Knowledge Management

The only question is, should an internal capability be built, should the capability be supported by contractors, or should the entire function be outsourced? Generally, core competencies are never outsourced, and expensive vendors often confer a significant cost advantage to in-house development. But the bottom line is, don't do it internally unless you intend to be good at it.

Monitor and Analyze Performance

The success criteria and other related measures for assessing performance should have been finalized/stabilized earlier in the knowledge management implementation process. These metrics should cover a broad range of external and internal measures. You may want to add measures as needed to cover special areas of need or interest. In addition to measuring performance in individual categories, you may want to compute an overall index of performance. Each measurement category is assigned a normalized weight based on relative importance, and then the product of the measure and weight are summarized across the categories, resulting in a balanced scorecard.

The external measures focus on customer requirements and the product/service characteristics that satisfy those requirements. In addition, customer needs, complaints, and problems can nearly always be expressed in terms of product and service features. The product category can be further divided into the following features:

- Functionality
- Quality
- Ease of use/learning
- Ease of repair
- Flexibility/customization
- Cost
- Convenience/ease of interactions

The service category can be further divided into the following features:

- Access to product, service, and cost information
- Transaction: contract, options, financing
- Delivery/installation
- Training/support
- Repair/maintenance/enhancement
- Timeliness/responsiveness
- Quality/expertise
- Cost

The internal measures focus primarily on business performance, rather than customer value and satisfaction. The internal measurement categories are:

- Process
- Financial
- Resource availability and utilization
- Workforce satisfaction

The process measures can be further decomposed into:

- Time
- Quality
- Cost
- Productivity
- Capacity

One potent measure of cycle time performance is the ratio of actual work time to total time elapsed (actual + wait times). Large improvements to operational efficiency can often be made here. Measures of quality include % reworks and customer satisfaction. Activity-Based Costing can be used to measure costs. Determine the cost performance by computing the ratio of value-added costs to total costs (value-added costs + non-value-added costs).

For most routine, high volume processes, measurement will be an ongoing, daily activity. For more unstructured, low volume processes, measurement frequency might be weekly or monthly, or by project. Once this operational data has been collected, an index of performance can be computed.

Analysis of measurement data relies on several concepts: trends, variation, seasonality. Trend analysis tells you the direction of the measure (up or down), and attempts to predict the future direction of a measure based on its historical trend (higher or lower). Variation is computed using techniques from Statistical Process Control. The intent is to minimize the variation, resulting in a more reliable, stable process. Seasonality is important both in operations as well as in human resources. For example, by knowing the historical annual peak volumes and their timing, much better planning, scheduling, and resource utilization can be achieved, thereby increasing performance.

Suggested Readings

APQC *International Benchmarking Clearinghouse. Knowledge Management Study Final Report.* American Productivity & Quality Center. 1996.

Jones, P., Palmer, J., Osterweil, C., and Whitehead, D. *Delivering Exceptional Performance: Aligning the Potential of Organizations, Teams and Individuals.* Pitman Publishing. 1996.

Leonard-Barton, D. *Wellsprings of Knowledge: Building and Sustaining the Sources of Innovation.* Harvard Business School Press. 1995.

Marquardt, M. *Building the Learning Organization.* McGraw–Hill. 1996.

Martin, J. *The Great Transition: Using the Seven Disciplines of Enterprise Engineering to Align People, Technology, and Strategy.* AMACOM. 1995.

McGill, M. and Slocum, J. *The Smarter Organization: How to Build a Business That Learns and Adapts to Marketplace Needs.* John Wiley & Sons. 1994.

Price Waterhouse Change Integration Team. *The Paradox Principles: How High-Performance Companies Manage Chaos, Complexity, and Contradiction to Achieve Superior Results.* Irwin. 1996.

Spitzer, D. *Super-Motivation: A Blueprint for Energizing Your Organization from Top to Bottom.* AMACOM. 1995.

Tobin, D. *Transformational Learning: Renewing Your Company through Knowledge and Skills.* John Wiley. 1996.

Vollmann, T. *The Transformation Imperative: Achieving Market Dominance through Radical Change.* Harvard Business School Press. 1996.

References

1. Jaworski, B. in Kahaner, L. *Competitive Intelligence: From Black Ops to Boardrooms — How Businesses Gather, Analyze, and Use Information to Succeed in the Global Marketplace.* Pages 33-34. Simon & Schuster. 1996.
2. Kaplan, R. and Norton, D. "Using the Balanced Scorecard as a Strategic Management System." *Harvard Business Review.* January–February 1996.
3. McGill, M. and Slocum, J. *The Smarter Organization: How to Build a Business That Learns and Adapts to Marketplace Needs.* John Wiley & Sons. 1994.
4. Rifkin, G. "Buckman Labs: Nothing but Net." *Fast Company.* June–July 1996.
5. Martin, J. *The Great Transition: Using the Seven Disciplines of Enterprise Engineering to Align People, Technology, and Strategy.* AMACOM. 1995.
6. Tobin, D. *Transformational Learning: Renewing Your Company through Knowledge and Skills.* John Wiley. 1996.
7. Kahaner, L. *Competitive Intelligence: From Black Ops to Boardrooms — How Businesses Gather, Analyze, and Use Information to Succeed in the Global Marketplace.* Simon & Schuster. 1996.
8. Prahalad, C.K., and Hamel, G. "The Core Competence of the Corporation." *Harvard Business Review*, 68, no. 3. 1990.
9. Beckman, T. *Implementing the Knowledge Organization in Government* presentation. 10th National Conference on Federal Quality. 1997.
10. Davenport, T. "Coming Soon: The CKO." *TechWeb*, CMP Media Inc. Sept. 5, 1994.
11. Davenport, T. "Some Principles of Knowledge Management." *Strategy*, Management, Competition. Winter, 1996.
12. Naumann, E. *Creating Customer Value: The Path to Sustainable Competitive Advantage.* Thompson Executive Press. 1995.
13. Beckman, T. *Applying AI to Business Reengineering* tutorial. Third World Congress on Expert Systems. Seoul, Korea. 1996.
14. Dalrymple, D. and Parsons, L. *Basic Marketing Management.* John Wiley & Sons Inc. 1995.
15. Beckman, T. *Creating a Self-Directed Work Team.* White paper. IRS. 1996.
16. APQC International Benchmarking Clearinghouse. *Knowledge Management Study Final Report.* American Productivity & Quality Center. 1996.

12 Future Knowledge Organizations

The future ain't what it used to be.

— Yogi Berra

We have had the database age, then the information age, and we are now entering the knowledge or artificial intelligence (AI) age. But what's ahead beyond artificial intelligence? No one knows for sure, but some educated guesses can be made. What we can look forward to in the year 2005 and beyond is the age of human-machine symbiosis.

The thrust of the age of human-machine symbiosis is that technological advancements will be made, probably not at the rate of technological achievements during previous ages, but the influence of this age is getting comfortable marriages of human and machine in the home, office, and play. Computers will become more powerful, more portable, more "user-friendly", and more "intelligent" in the coming years, but the emphasis in the year 2005 will be on the relationship between human and machine in integrating the machine more into everyday activities. The emphasis in 2005 will be not merely on technology, but more on the symbiotic relationship between humans and computers, as a part of life.

Integrating computers into one's environment should not be too difficult. Today, elementary age students are using computers in school and at home. For these individuals, computers are already a part of their lives. These kids are familiar with computers, using them for games and education. By the year 2005, these kids will be close to college age, and will have had numerous courses on computers in school. They will be very acclimated to computers through their usage in school, at home, and at video arcades. A synergistic effect between person and computers will be built, and the computer will

181

become a necessary tool of everyday life. We will have to work with robots in automobile assembly lines; voice input to word processing will be used; and many games and tools will incorporate microchip technology. Computers will become a greater part of everyone's life, and as more people learn about computers from elementary school on up, they will accept them more and use them comfortably.

Technologically speaking, the age of human-machine symbiosis will bring about new and interesting technological achievements. Wristwatches that serve as telephones for both speaking and sending written messages might be very affordable and commonplace by the year 2005. Machines that can understand what one is speaking and then automatically transcribe those words might be very commonplace in businesses by the year 2005. Natural language interfaces to bibliographic retrieval systems might be commonplace by 2005, so that one can easily search for information in libraries. With laser technology, new discoveries in medical operating procedures will be realized by the year 2005 or sooner. Computer vision will be improved so that robots will become more capable in industry and at home. FAX machines for sending documents and pictures, which are already prevalent in many businesses, will be commonplace in many homes by the year 2005. In fact, some indicate that by the year 2000, one-third of all American homes will have a fax machine, or images will be sent directly to personal computers, bypassing paper altogether.

As these technological advancements take place, a central issue will be integrating these new inventions, at an affordable price, into society. For example, as more robots infiltrate the assembly lines, two key questions result: First, what happens to the individuals that they are replacing, and second, how does one manage these robots and integrate them into a workplace shared by both people and robots? The first question suggests that some new technology will eliminate jobs of others. This means that there will have to be a retraining or retooling program for those whose jobs were eliminated by machines, like robots. The second question deals with the management issue of having robots in the workforce. This centers around finding ways of having workers feel comfortable around robots. This is one example of the upcoming age of human-machine symbiosis.

The Future of Knowledge Systems Technology

Knowledge organizations will use expert systems technology as an integral part of their operations. According to Hayes-Roth:[1]

We envision a world filled with millions of knowledge agents, advisers, and assistants. The integration between human knowledge agents and machine agents will be seamless, often making it difficult to know which is which.

We envision a world in which people publish active electronic knowledge and get paid each time it is used. This will be accomplished by instrumenting knowledge systems and making them widely available on high-bandwidth computer and communication networks.

Innovative companies are already regularly capturing and reapplying their knowledge in design, manufacturing, sales, and service delivery. Knowledge is being built into all kinds of products, from automobiles to microwave ovens to vacuum cleaners. This process is accelerating due to the advent of interactive electronic books, personal digital assistants, and integrated fax, telephone, and wireless computing and communication devices. We envision a wide variety of publicly available commercial services and industrial processes that exploit ubiquitous and diverse knowledge systems.[1: p. 38]

Knowledge sharing will also be a critical element in building knowledge organizations. Incentive systems to encourage knowledge sharing are needed, as well as the conceptual and technological advances in developing the bridges between the islands of knowledge.

Data mining and knowledge discovery will also play an essential role in further developing knowledge organizations. These technologies involve finding useful patterns in data. According to Brachman et al.,[2] domains suitable for knowledge discovery are information-rich, have a changing environment, do not already have existing models, require knowledge-based decisions, and provide high payoff for the right decisions.

The future knowledge organization will use an "integrated" approach to doing business. Through the use of employee knowledge profiles, they will assemble the "best" internal, multidisciplinary teams to handle their business transactions and client engagements. They will tap into their knowledge repositories and global case bases to learn how similar assignments were handled and solved. They will use their company intranets and knowledge management exchange tools to access, store, and retrieve important information, knowledge, and heuristics relating to their situation or business activity. Expert systems also will play a major role in providing an active advisory component to the organization's knowledge repositories and corporate memory. Integrated Performance Support Systems, supported by Knowledge Repositories, may just turn out to be the breakthrough concepts needed to implement this integrated approach.

Companies will need to cure their "corporate amnesia" in order to maintain their competitive edge. Organizations will probably continue to merge, reengineer, downsize, and flatten. As a direct result, a turnover of employees will be created which could result in a brain drain effect. To overcome this potential problem, knowledge repositories must be created and maintained to capture the expertise before people leave. In concert with these trends, future organizations may well need to be more focused and specialized in their business strategies, relaying on alliances and partnerships to produce products and deliver services that the previously would have performed internally.

According to Robert Dunham of Enterprise Design:

> The power of incorporating action into our interpretation of knowledge is that it puts the focus on the actions to be produced, not just on understanding or information that requires another step to get to action. Understanding and information are still aspects of knowledge, but they are no longer the end product.[4]

Organizations need to be proactive, and put knowledge into action. It's "action" that produces value for customers. According to Laurence Prusak of IBM/Ernst & Young, the only thing that gives an organization a competitive edge — the only thing that is sustainable — is what it knows, how it uses what it knows, and how fast it can know something new.[5] This "knowledge advantage" will be a major competitive advantage for the organization in years to come.

According to Brook Manville, Director of Knowledge Management at McKinsey & Company, and Nathaniel Foote, McKinsey's Director of Knowledge and Practice Development, the following advice is given:[3]

- Knowledge-based strategies begin with strategy, not knowledge. A company has to know the kind of value it intends to provide and to whom. Only then can it link its knowledge resources in ways that make a difference.
- Knowledge-based strategies aren't strategies unless you can link them to traditional measures of performance. If knowledge can't be connected to measurable improvements in performance — including improvements on the bottom line — then the knowledge revolution will be short-lived.
- Executing a knowledge-based strategy is not about managing knowledge; it's about nurturing people with knowledge. Also, people will not willingly share it with coworkers if their workplace culture does not support learning, cooperation, and openness.

- Organizations leverage knowledge through networks of people who collaborate — not through networks of technology that interconnect.
- People networks leverage knowledge through organization "pull" rather than centralized information "push."

Organizations will need to continue developing their "organizational intelligence." Organizational intelligence is an organization's capability to process, interpret, encode, manipulate, and access information in a purposeful, goal-directed manner, so it can increase its adaptive potential in the environment in which it operates.[7] Organizational intelligence is a social outcome and is related to individual intelligence by mechanisms of aggregation, cross-level transference, and distribution.[7] Knowledge management methodologies, techniques, and tools can facilitate the development of organizational intelligence. Organizational roles, like the Chief Knowledge Officer or Chief Learning Officer, can both develop and diffuse intelligence in the organization. Technologies, like Management Information System and expert systems, can also facilitate organizational learning and enable the development of organizational intelligence. Much organizational wisdom and managerial knowledge can be captured and stored in knowledge repositories and databases.

Knowledge and Skills in 2010

The Plasschaert Quality in Research (PQR) in Amsterdam interviewed forty people, from children to elders, to find out what knowledge and skills will be needed in the year 2010. Of interest to knowledge management were two questions:[6]

- What knowledge and skills do people think it will be desirable for ordinary members of society to possess in 2010?
- How and where could and should such knowledge and skills be acquired?

All respondents indicated that "being socially minded" was the key in having communications and social skills in 2010. In terms of knowledge, a broad general education is expected to be of such importance that nobody will be able to operate as a full member of society without it. Social knowledge is also critical including:[6]

- a knowledge of the background and culture of social minorities, which will increase understanding of and respect for others.
- communication skills, essential to enable individuals to function both at work and in the everyday life of society.
- specialized (vocational) knowledge, including knowledge of management skills, of computers (both for software development and for the use of applications), of specific trades, and connections with the caring professions.

Respondents identified five major learning situations within which the knowledge and skills needed to cope with the society of 2010 could/should be acquired:[6]

- the family
- the local community
- the education system
- the world of work, or the business world
- individual leisure time.

Two general themes were identified. First, the role of parents, of the business world, and of the individual's own leisure time will increase in importance due to declining public educational provision and as a result of increasing company demands for specialist knowledge and the increasing amount of leisure time. The second common theme suggested that the role of the education system and the local community will decline.[6] There will be much more workplace training (learning by doing) by companies. There will be a continued need for lifelong learning to increase the chance of obtaining and staying in employment. Additionally, "social upbringing" will have to be reinforced, with attention being paid to the inculcation of norms and values and the teaching of social and communication skills.[6]

========================= VIGNETTE =========================

Putting Knowledge Discovery Technologies into Business Practice (Some Examples)

Marketing:

Coverstory and Spotlight are two systems which analyze supermarket sales data and produce reports (using natural language and business graphics) on the most significant changes in a particular product volume and share broken down by region, product type, and other dimensions. Spotlight later grew into the Opportunity Explorer system which supports sales representatives of consumer packaged-goods companies in examining their business with individual retailers.

Financial Investment:
The Fidelity Stock Selector fund uses neural network models to select investments. LBS Capital Management, a fund management firm, uses expert systems, neural nets, and genetic algorithms to manage portfolios worth $600 million; since its introduction in 1993, the system has outperformed the overall stock market.

Fraud Detection:
The FALCON fraud assessment system from HNC Inc. was developed using a neural network shell and is now used by many retail banks to detect suspicious credit card transactions. The Financial Crimes Enforcement Network AI System (FAIS) helps the U.S. Treasury identify financial transactions that may indicate money laundering activity. AT&T developed the Clonedetector system for detecting international calling fraud by displaying calling activity in a way that lets users quickly see unusual patterns.

Manufacturing and Production:
General Electric and SNECMA developed the CASSIOPEE system to diagnose and predict problems in Boeing 737 aircraft. The Telecommunication Alarm Sequence Analyzer (TASA) was built at the University of Helsinki to locate frequently occurring alarm episodes from the alarm stream and produce valuable information about the behavior of the network.

Source: Ronald Brachman, T. Khabaza, W. Kloesgen, G. Piatetsky–Shapiro, and E. Simoudis, "Mining Business Databases," *Communications of the ACM*, Vol. 39, No. 11, Association for Computing Machinery, New York, November 1996.

Conclusions

Artificial intelligence deals with developing intelligent computer power to supplement human brain power, and better understanding how we think, learn, and reason. The age of artificial intelligence that we are just approaching promises us some exciting new technologies. At that time, we believe that many of these technologies will be affordable and accepted for use in the office and home. By the year 2005, an age of human-machine symbiosis will appear whose focus will be to easily integrate these new technologies into the workplace and home, and to have individuals feel comfortable in using these technologies. If costs of these products drop and if acceptance of these technologies grows, then the age of human-machine symbiosis might indeed bring us knowledge-based ovens, knowledge organizations, and wristwatch telephones in daily use by 2005 or earlier!

References

1. Hayes-Roth, F., "The State of Knowledge-Based Systems," *Communications of the ACM*, Association for Computing Machinery, March 1994.
2. Brachman, R., T. Khabaza, W. Kloesgen, G. Shapiro, and E. Simoudis, "Mining Business Databases," *Communications of the ACM*, Association for Computing Machinery, November 1996.
3. Manville, B. And N. Foote, "Strategy As If Knowledge Mattered," *FastCompany Newsletter*, 1996, http://www.fastcompany.com/fastco/Issues/Second/Strat-Sec.htm.
4. Dunham, R., "Knowledge in Action — The New Business Battleground," *KM Briefs*, May 1, 1996, http://www.ktic.com/topic6/KMBATTLE.HTM.
5. Prusak, L., "The Knowledge Advantage," *Strategy & Leadership Journal*, March–April 1996.
6. Plasschaert Quality in Research, *Knowledge for Tomorrow: Forty Interviews*, Amsterdam, The Netherlands, 1996, http://www.kennisdebat.minocw.nl/papers/forty_e.htm#2010.
7. Glynn, M.A., "Innovative Genius: A Framework for Relating Individual and Organizational Intelligences to Innovation," *Academy of Management Review*, Vol. 21, No. 4, October 1996.

INDEX

189

For Product Safety Concerns and Information please contact our EU
representative GPSR@taylorandfrancis.com
Taylor & Francis Verlag GmbH, Kaufingerstraße 24, 80331 München, Germany

www.ingramcontent.com/pod-product-compliance
Ingram Content Group UK Ltd.
Pitfield, Milton Keynes, MK11 3LW, UK
UKHW021825240425
457818UK00006B/74